Your
Teacher Said
WHAT?!

Your Teacher Said WHAT?!

Defending Our Kids from the Liberal Assault on Capitalism

Joe Kernen

and

Blake Kernen

Sentinel

SENTINEL
Published by the Penguin Group
Penguin Group (USA) Inc., 375 Hudson Street,
New York, New York 10014, U.S.A.
Penguin Group (Canada), 90 Eglinton Avenue East, Suite 700,
Toronto, Ontario, Canada M4P 2Y3
(a division of Pearson Penguin Canada Inc.)
Penguin Books Ltd, 80 Strand, London WC2R 0RL, England
Penguin Ireland, 25 St. Stephen's Green, Dublin 2, Ireland
(a division of Penguin Books Ltd)
Penguin Books Australia Ltd, 250 Camberwell Road, Camberwell,
Victoria 3124, Australia
(a division of Pearson Australia Group Pty Ltd)
Penguin Books India Pvt Ltd, 11 Community Centre, Panchsheel Park,
New Delhi – 110 017, India
Penguin Group (NZ), 67 Apollo Drive, Rosedale, Auckland 0632,
New Zealand (a division of Pearson New Zealand Ltd)
Penguin Books (South Africa) (Pty) Ltd, 24 Sturdee Avenue,
Rosebank, Johannesburg 2196, South Africa

Penguin Books Ltd, Registered Offices:
80 Strand, London WC2R 0RL, England

First published in 2011 by Sentinel,
a member of Penguin Group (USA) Inc.

10 9 8 7 6 5 4 3 2 1

LIBRARY OF CONGRESS CATALOGING IN PUBLICATION DATA
Kernen, Joe.
Your teacher said what?! : defending our kids from the liberal assault on capitalism / Joe Kernen and
Blake Kernen.
    p.   cm.
    Includes bibliographical references and index.
    ISBN 978-1-59523-077-5
    1. Capitalism—United States.   2. Free enterprise—United States.   3. United States—Economic
conditions—2009–.   4. United States—Economic policy—2009–.   I. Kernen, Blake, 1999–.
II. Title.
HB501.K458 2011
330.12'20973—dc22   2011005036

Printed in the United States of America
Set in Adobe Caslon Pro
Designed by Spring Hoteling

To Penelope

Contents

Preface
The Complaint Department

It took me twenty years to find something about America really worth ranting about.

Oh, I ranted anyway. A lot. I grumbled about brain-challenged bureaucrats at every level of government and about the jug-headed legislators who employ them. I fumed about the policies of the Federal Reserve, about the accountants at the Social Security Administration, and about everything related to health-care reform and global warming. I even whined about the incomprehensible forms used for everything from insurance claims to travel reimbursement. And as is the sacred right of all Americans, I groused long and eloquently about taxes.

But I didn't actually have anything all that awful to complain about, since for nearly the entire twenty years I was getting paid to share my rants about the world's largest and freest economy. I got to talk about business and the economy with everyone from billionaire industrialist Warren Buffett to former Treasury secretary Hank Paulson. I met with the country's—the world's!—smartest investors and economists during the greatest bull market in history and the biggest economic crisis since the Great Depression. And I got to do so in front of an audience who watches me on television with a devotion that borders on the obsessive. They watch so carefully, in fact, that hundreds of them send me e-mails every day, agreeing with me, disagreeing with me, or telling me how I've entirely missed the point.* You may be one of them. If you're tired of hearing me complain, I understand.

But if so, you should stop reading now. Because a couple of years ago, I found the first truly worthwhile reason to rant about the economy. It wasn't unfunded mandates, Medicare insolvency, CEO compensation, or the federal deficit.

It was one nine-year-old girl. And that same girl—by the time you read this, she'll be eleven, going on twenty—is the reason for this book.

She's not what I rant about, of course. From the day Blake Alexandra Kernen was born, the day after Christmas in 1999, she's done hardly anything worth complaining about. This didn't mean that she never made her mother and me fret. Like any new father, when I wasn't overwhelmed by the sheer terror of it all (in my case, terror amplified by the fact that I had become a father for the first time in my mid-forties), I was worrying plenty: Was a temperature of 100 degrees worth a call to the doctor or a trip to the hospital? Was she walking early enough? Too early? Did she have enough playdates? *Too* many?

By the time Blake's brother, Scott Joseph, showed up two years later, I was an old hand at worrying. In fact, by then I had found an entirely new and durable thing to worry about. Like any father, I worried about whether I would measure up—whether I would succeed in doing for Blake and Scott what my parents had done for me: giving them the values that reflected what their mother and I cherished most. We wanted our kids to believe in God, love their country, and respect the principles of hard work and fairness. We

---

* Or even making comments about my waistline on the CNBC Web site, which really hurt.

wanted them to value honesty, courage, and kindness, to be polite and respectful.

Simple, right? After all, these principles are widely shared in twenty-first-century America. Our church teaches us that we are obliged to care for people who can't care for themselves; our schools reward hard work and demand respect. Kids learn good sportsmanship from playing tennis and soccer. The heroes of their favorite movies and television programs are generally pretty brave (though occasionally a little goofy; SpongeBob, anyone?).

With one exception. Penelope and I are capitalists—and not just because we've done pretty well out of the capitalist system. We believe that free-market capitalism is not only the most powerful engine for human prosperity ever but also history's strongest force for freedom and human advancement. We believe—no, we *know*—that economic freedom is as important as religious freedom or freedom of speech. We believe that productive work, freely exchanged, is a virtue, just like charity freely given.

Please don't misunderstand this. We're not teaching Blake and Scott that their purpose in life is to get as rich as possible; it's to make sure that everyone is as *free* as possible. For us, the only difference between defending economic freedom and defending religious freedom is that while the mainstream culture offers no real opposition to the many ways in which Americans worship, there is a powerful current of antagonism toward the ways in which they do business.

Some of the attacks on free-market capitalism are overt: the idea, for example, that capitalism is unavoidably brutal, or at least immoral. Some are of the more-in-sorrow-than-anger category, such as the notion that we should increase the benefits of the free market by taxing and regulating it into submission. Many are specific to the issues of the moment, like the idea that the best solution to the unsustainable growth of entitlements like Social Security and Medicare is to make them grow even faster (you can't make up some of this stuff).

And *that* is something worth ranting about: not anything my kids do, but what is being done to them.

Consider that, during Blake's first ten years, the United States of America not only elected a Republican president who increased the nation's debt by more than $4 trillion—yes: that's trillion, with a *T*—and a Democrat who is certain to break even that dubious record but experienced the worst economic disaster since the Chicago Cubs were a dynasty.* About the only constant of those ten years, in fact, is that trust in the free-enterprise system seemed to sink lower in every one of them.

The country, of course, is still suffering from a loss of faith in free markets. But at least in the Kernen household, it doesn't have to incapacitate us. Which is why we decided to spend a year—it turned into nearly two—taking the antidote: a daily (okay, not daily—but nearly) dose of free-market philosophy.

It started with asking Blake to start writing down words and phrases she heard but didn't understand about the economy, politics, and so on. Some of them seemed complicated but weren't ("What's physical stimulus?") and some seemed simple but were really complicated ("I already *know* what a price is!"). Some of Blake's questions led me to discover ideas I didn't know about already, like the Higgs effect: the way that governments manage to turn temporary crises into permanent programs. And sometimes her answers served to remind me that she was still, after all, ten years old (with Blake, you constantly need to remind yourself of this). The idea of credit, for example, led naturally to an attempt to explain that money has a time value, that a dollar today is worth more than a dollar a year from now. Not, it turns out, to someone whose purchases are entirely subsidized by someone else.

What else? Blake and I learned something about the origins of

---

* Bad as the Great Depression was for the country, it was a golden age for the Cubs: Between 1929 and 1939, they won the National League pennant five times. On the other hand, they didn't win the World Series even once; they were, after all, still the Cubs.

the Progressive movement in America, and the fact that its strongest political component has always been labor unions. This is not a coincidence: Progressivism *always* prefers collective endeavors to individual ones, and the biggest collectivists in the American economy are the ones whose whole reason for being is—wait for it—collective bargaining. Unfortunately, they are also the adults our children spend the most hours a day with, and we spend a lot of time talking about the pluses (small) and minuses (humongous) of unionism, from the plumbers who fix our furnace to the teachers who wonder aloud about the benefits of the free-enterprise system that pays their salaries.

There was more: Tea partiers in the United States versus socialist rioters in Europe; the sinister side of food propaganda—I swear I didn't know what "locavorism" was before, and am still not sure it wasn't made up as a joke—and the huge significance of property rights for not just prosperity but freedom itself. And if you're anything like me, I can guarantee that your jaw will drop the same way mine did once I started paying attention to the hostility to free-market capitalism that infects almost every movie and television show your kids are watching.

We had fun. One of our favorites was following the complicated process by which even the simplest manufactured item gets made, all without anyone directing it from above. Free markets can be pretty elegant to watch in action. And we had a bit of torture: For a month, Blake and I compared the editorial pages from the *New York Times* with those of the *Wall Street Journal*, stopping just this side of child endangerment.

Blake didn't always agree with Penelope and me. One thing I learned is that the most powerful way in which nine- or ten-year-olds resemble grown-up Progressives is in their love of regulating things. There's just no way Blake can see something that's not good for you—like smoking cigarettes, or eating too much fast food—without wanting a law to ban it. I can only hope that she outgrows this before too long . . . but I also notice that the mayor of New York City (a man I otherwise admire) has this notion so firmly planted in his head that he is proposing a ban on cigarette smoking in the "crossroads of the world"—that part of Times Square where tourists sit at tables in the middle of one street while a hundred thousand vehicles are belching exhaust a few yards away. Progressivism is a durable bit of craziness.

So is parenting. Trying to plant the seeds of what we hope will be a lifelong philosophy in a ten-year-old brain is an alternately satisfying and frustrating assignment, and the time that Blake and I have been embarked on this father-and-daughter exercise has taught me that educating a child in the way free markets are supposed to work (and, most of the time, the way they actually *do* work) has never been harder . . . or more rewarding.

If you already have kids, you already know this. And if you don't . . . well, don't say I didn't warn you.

A Note from Blake

Hi. I'm Blake Kernen and I want to thank you so much for reading this book. Writing this book was an incredible learning experience. I discussed many topics with my dad that most fifth graders don't even know about but probably should. Here are some things I learned while working on this book.

> I learned about our bank. It's a lot more than just a building. And I learned that "credit" means "trust."

> Sometimes it's better to take a chance on choosing something that *might* lose but also *might* succeed. I even learned how to figure out how much it would have to succeed to make choosing it a good idea.

> In my opinion, it doesn't make a lot of sense to buy all your food just because it's grown locally. In Holland, they have something called "graffiti eggplant" which are purple and

white. If we had to buy everything locally, no Holland egg-plants. (This is one of the good things about trade: *Everybody* makes something good, and trade is how everyone can do what they do best.)

People shouldn't all be paid the same, no matter how hard they work.

Sometimes a house is a kind of property. And sometimes it isn't. (Actually, I learned that there are tons of different kinds of property. Like this book is *your* property, if you bought it; but the right to copy the words in it isn't. This is called "copyright.")

I learned that the difference between free markets and not-free markets isn't like turning on a lightbulb. The economy (this is everything that everyone buys and sells) is more like a dimmer switch: The brighter it gets, the freer people are.

People sometimes forget that something that's good (like saving wild animals or helping the environment) can also be bad (because it means that people aren't allowed to work).

Also, I learned two things about free markets. The first thing is that even if you took the hundred smartest people in the world and gave them the hundred most powerful computers, they still wouldn't be able to figure out what people want to buy and sell. When I go to the store to buy a net for my aquarium (I have puffer fish), I can find a lot of nets on the shelf, but no one told the store which ones to put on the shelf, and no one told the companies that make the nets how many to make, and no one told the companies that deliver the nets when to bring them to the store. Or rather, *everyone* told them. Which is why millions of ordinary people deciding what to buy and sell are smarter than even the hundred smartest people in the world.

The second thing I learned is that when something isn't free, it's like property, and you can do whatever you want (mostly) with your property. Like a farmer can tell his cows where they can go and what they can eat because they're his property. But people aren't cows. And in my opinion, we should mostly leave them alone, to make up their own minds how hard to work and what to buy and sell.

That's what free markets are.

In elementary school we learned about our forefathers and the great sacrifices they made that allow us to live the way we do. George Washington and his army marched right through my own township in pursuit of freedom for Americans. The Declaration of Independence states that all Americans have the right to life, liberty, and the pursuit of happiness. I believe I have a better understanding of what that really means after working on this book.

Oh, and here's another lesson I learned: I will never complain about another homework assignment again. This was definitely the longest assignment in my life, so far.

Your
Teacher Said
WHAT?!

CHAPTER I

January 2009: The Progressive Slot Machine

By January 2009, the Great Recession had been going on for more than a year; the U.S. government was about to take over Chrysler and General Motors, unemployment was through the roof, and the stock market had fallen by more than 40 percent. There was no shortage of reasons to be angry, but at least none of them affected my kids. Or so I thought . . .

"Dad?"
"Yes, Blake?"
"What's a recession?"

I didn't think that my then-nine-year-old daughter wanted the technical answer—two consecutive quarters of negative GDP growth. Or maybe I just didn't want to have to explain that day what GDP stands for, much less how it's calculated.

"A recession is when the economy stops growing and starts shrinking."
"Economy?"
I should have known better.

"The economy is the sum of all the buying and selling that goes on in America. All the stuff we buy and sell, like food and clothes and cars and houses and such; and all the work we do, and we pay for, like your tennis camp or your guitar teacher. When we buy and sell more stuff and services in this year than we did last year, then the economy is growing; when we buy less, it's in recession."

"My teacher says the recession is the banks' fault."

"That's way too simple, Blake. For something as big as this recession, there's a lot of blame to go around."

"And my teacher says it's 'cause we care too much about buying stuff, and it might not be so bad if we stopped."

"Your teacher said . . . *what*?"

The Great Recession was a wake-up call for everyone, but this exchange had the same effect as a bathtub full of ice water falling on my head. I was panicked at the thought that my very smart young daughter had fallen prey to a media culture and an educational system that were not only completely ignorant of the nature of a free-market economy but, often enough, hostile to it. It was as if I had learned that she was being taught geology by a member of the Flat Earth Society.

How long had this been going on? Probably since the day Blake began kindergarten and started being exposed to the economic philosophies of adults other than her mother and me. But I didn't really think about how to respond until January 20, 2009.

When Barack Hussein Obama took the oath of office, I admit I understood the proud cheers of the hundreds of thousands of people lining the parade route in Washington that day. I didn't vote for the guy, but I'm not a complete dolt, and I could see how his election said something pretty positive about America. Pundit after pundit had spent the preceding weeks reminding me that this was something that couldn't have happened anywhere else, and if they had drunk just a little too much of the Obama Kool-Aid, they weren't completely wrong. A black man with, shall we say, a foreign-sounding name had just been elected the leader of the free world. You can get pretty drunk on that sort of stuff.

The hangover didn't take long coming. And it's gotten so bad since that I can't even see an Obama bumper sticker without getting the headache, dry mouth, and general depression all over again.

My hangover isn't the result of concerns about the president's birth certificate. Or worries that he is some kind of Manchurian candidate in the pay of a foreign power. I don't think he is Muslim, or racist, or anticolonialist, or un-American. I don't blame him for the Troubled Asset Relief Program, which was passed by the previous administration (and which, given the circumstances, I actually thought was needed). And while I don't agree with all his foreign-policy decisions—okay, with any of them—I know he inherited a pretty poor set of options, and also that I don't really know enough about Iraq or Afghanistan or Iran to second-guess everything that is happening there.

No, my problems with the president are on an entirely different plane: I hate what he's doing to my children's future, and I don't have to think that Barack Obama is the devil to know that he has a very different idea than I do about what America should look like when Blake and Scott are adults.

It's a belief thing. Penelope and I believe in free markets—that the best economic decisions are made by the largest number of individuals acting in what they believe to be their own interests. President Obama and most of his administration believe in an economy that depends on the cleverest people acting in what they believe to be the interests of everyone else. We believe in voluntary associations. They prefer compulsory ones, at least when it comes to health insurance or union organizing.

One thing they don't care much for is business. Like a lot of people, I test out a lot of my thinking by talking things over with my friends. One of them is also one of *Squawk Box*'s favorite guests, and not just because he was the CEO of CNBC's parent company from the time the network was founded until he retired—as the most admired businessman in America—in 2001.

Jack Welch isn't sure *why* the current administration is antibusiness but doesn't doubt that it is. *Really* antibusiness. And really intimidating. Here's what Jack had to say on *Squawk Box* back in September 2010:

> Right off the bat, Joe, he's in office one month, and what does he do? He vilifies Las Vegas, as a place "fat cats" go to conventions. Now, first off, "fat cats" don't go to conventions; *salesmen* go to conventions, which doesn't show a lot of understanding. And what's the result: He hammers both the travel industry *and* the sales business.
>
> Then he bails out the auto industry, and the company's bondholders get smashed—he called them "speculators"—and hands GM and Chrysler over to the United Auto Workers.
>
> Then, after the Supreme Court decided, in the Citizens United ruling, that corporations can spend money on campaigns in the same way unions already do, the president, in the State of the Union, ridicules the members of the court for their so-called probusiness ruling.

I asked him, "Why doesn't the administration see the disconnect between what you call antibusiness sentiment and what I'm sure is their real desire to add jobs?"

"Maybe they're bipolar. Or maybe it's sleight of hand."

It doesn't stop there. The president, and those sympathetic to him, follow the liberal philosopher John Rawls, who used to argue that the best society was the one you'd pick from behind a "veil of ignorance," the one you'd design if you didn't know whether you'd be born rich or poor and were determined to make sure that being born poor wouldn't be so bad. Penelope and I, on the other hand, believe in a "window of optimism": that the best society is the one that gives people the best chance to achieve. They think property rights are in conflict with human rights; we think property rights *are* human rights. They believe in the tax system as a way of promoting desirable social goals, like reduced inequality; we think taxes are just a method for funding necessary—*necessary*—government activity.

What do you call these people? Once upon a time, I would have called them liberals, and most everyone would have understood what that meant. However, one of the consequences of spending some time in the company of Adam Smith, Friedrich Hayek, and Ludwig von Mises is being reminded that that the word "liberal" used to mean something very different: an affection for liberty, free markets, and property rights, along with a hostility to economic cronyism.

Pretty confusing, no?

I'm a little happier calling them "Progressives." Partly this is because that's what they've taken to calling themselves, but mostly it's because the history of progressivism—excuse me, Progressivism—really explains the two sides in this battle a whole lot better.

People have been calling themselves "progressives" in America since the end of the nineteenth century and mostly started out with a laudable interest in improving the lot of the poor. Progressives built schools and settlement houses, ran charities, fought corruption in government, and recruited the Bull Moose himself, Theodore Roosevelt, who ran for president in 1912 as—you guessed it—the candidate of the Progressive Party. But the soul of Progressivism was a journalist named Herbert Croly, who published a book called *The Promise of American Life* in 1909.

If you want to understand modern Progressives—and especially the Progressive wing of the Democratic party—you could do a lot worse than reading Croly. Here are a few of his choicest observations about America:

"American history contains much matter for pride and congratulation, and much matter for regret and humiliation."

America was "saved from the consequences of its distracting individualistic conception of democracy."

"The popular will cannot be taken for granted, it must be created."

In order to govern, according to Croly, people must be shown that the "special interests" really run things, that the pursuit of profit by Haves (Croly's capitalization) is antidemocratic. It's not that Croly didn't like elites; he *loved* them, since the people didn't really understand their own best interests, and only powerful leaders could "accelerate the desirable process of social reconstruction."

However, Progressives, true to their heritage as do-gooders, greatly prefer their elites to be uncorrupted by anything as soul-destroying as money. Like, for example, the First Lady of the United States, Michelle Obama, who told a group of women at a day care center in Zanesville, Ohio, in 2008: "Don't go into corporate America. You know, become teachers. Work for the community. Be social workers. Be a nurse. Those are the careers that we need. But if you make that choice, as we did, to move out of the money-making industry into the helping industry, then your salaries respond."*

Or the president himself, who said in an interview with *Bloomberg BusinessWeek* about plans to curb the bonuses being paid to Haves in the financial services industry, "I, like most of the American people, don't begrudge people success or wealth. . . . I do think that the compensation packages that we've seen over the last decade at least have not matched up always to performance."

Well, everyone hates bankers. But hardware stores?

---

* Note that Mrs. Obama, who had traced her family's financial success to her husband's two best-selling books, earned $121,910 in 2004 . . . and after her husband was elected to the U.S. Senate in 2005, $316,962.

Bernie Marcus, one of the founders of Home Depot, is a regular guest on *Squawk Box*, and he sure knows when someone is insulting him. To the Obama administration, he says, people who create jobs "are monsters. We're disgusting human beings." His cofounder, Ken Langone, goes even further. He showed up at the president's town-hall meeting in September 2010 and asked him why, since a dynamic economy was so essential to growing the economy, he spent so much time vilifying the people who delivered that growth. The president responded that Ken was part of a group that had been "reckless." Who had made "bad decisions." And who needed "guidance" from Washington.

Sound familiar?

"Blake?"

"Yes, Dad?"

"Have you ever heard the word 'progressive'?"

"I think so."

"What do you think it means?"

"Maybe . . . something about progress?"

If only. Actually, Progressives have pretty mixed feelings about progress. While it's true that Progressives have long supported stuff that just about *everyone* would call progress—like woman suffrage and an end to racial discrimination—and even things that at least *some* people would call progress—like stronger environmental legislation— when it comes to policies that promote *material* progress (you know, improving people's wealth, choice, and living conditions), Progressives are usually the ones pulling back on the reins and yelling, "Whoa!"*

---

* This is actually one way that twenty-first-century century Progressives differ from their early-twentieth-century ancestors, who were eager to adopt labor-saving technologies, possibly because they still remembered the backbreaking labor associated with preindustrial farming and manufacturing. Whenever you hear the word "artisanal" spoken approvingly in reference to clothing or food, you are in the presence of a Progressive.

Partly this is because the typical Progressive hasn't got a clue about what actually produces wealth. This is a truism that turns out to be true, at least statistically: A study by the Federal Reserve Bank of New York clearly showed that the more economics classes you take in college, the less likely you are to support any part of the Progressive agenda. Breaking it down to the most basic kind of free-market thinking, this means that the more economics you know, the less likely you are to believe in the Progressive doctrine that tariffs are necessary to protect domestic jobs and that free trade hurts prosperity (it doesn't). The more you know about economics, the less likely you are to support the Progressive belief in higher minimum wages (they actually raise unemployment). And the greater your economic literacy, the less likely you are to buy the Progressive idea that governments should set prices or wages (sorry, but duh).

And, no surprise, Progressives *love* the Progressive (oops, I meant progressive) income tax. Almost as much as they love redistributing income in a way that meets their own definition of fairness, taking money from one group to pay another.

And speaking of taking money: In Las Vegas and other cities that use the mathematics of probability to separate customers from their cash, by far the most profitable "game" of chance is the one played one-on-one with slot machines: Put your money in here, and pray that more comes out there. At the very pinnacle of this one-armed banditry are payoffs that take a small percentage of the total amount of money played in a whole network of machines, tempting arithmetic-challenged players to keep pouring money into slots hoping for a million-dollar payday. Let me repeat that: a slot machine that takes money from *other* slot machines in order to promise a giant payday. The technical name for this sort of system: progressive slot machines.

Makes you think.

The Progressive opinions held by Blake's teachers shouldn't have come as a complete shock, but they did. Like most folks who earn a living in the world of business and finance, I spend my working day around people who take the virtues of free-market capitalism for granted. Partly this is a matter of temperament; planned-economy enthusiasts don't tend to look for jobs at CNBC. Really, though, it's the fact that people like me learned what we know about the real-world economy in, well, the real world. When you spend your days with people who are spending *their* days buying, selling, and trading, Adam Smith's "invisible hand" isn't some classroom abstraction; it's tapping you on your shoulder all day long.

For a lot of people, though (and all children), knowledge about how the economic world works is acquired elsewhere. From television dramas and comedies, for example, whose creators are so convinced of the evil of profit-making business that they depict its participants as many times more likely to commit murder or assault than, say, members of street gangs.

Or from newspapers and news magazines. When they're not tsk-tsking over something called "excess profits," they're declaring "Free Trade a Casualty of Economic Crisis" (*Washington Post*) or even wondering whether we've arrived at "The End of Capitalism?" (*Time* magazine; the question mark is a nice touch). *Time for Kids*, the elementary school edition of *Time*, even wrote that "lower interest rates give people comfort that government will do whatever it can to solve [this] crisis." *Time for Kids!* I guess it's not that shocking to find the Progressive buffet laid out in any version of *Time* magazine, but I admit I was a little surprised to see how ten-year-olds eat it up.

The reason, of course, is that ten-year-olds are natural Progressives.

Think about it: All of the components of the modern Progressive agenda are in sync with the way a parent tries to raise a child:

- Redistribution: We teach our children to share with others, to not be selfish.
- Regulation: We have rules to order every aspect of a child's life, from meal choices to bedtimes.

- Dependence: We tell our children that they will be taken care of, that we'll keep the bogeymen away.

That's what Penelope and I have taught Blake and Scott. It's what any decent parent tries to do. Progressivism, at its core, isn't really anything but the idea that the government ought to act like a parent.

The big difference, of course, is that we're trying to *raise* our children—to turn them into adults who can someday raise their own children. The Obamacrats in the White House, the Senate, and the House and a dizzying number of bureaucrats, obedient to their Progressive instincts, want to keep the American people children forever.

So when I tell you I'm ready to rant about what they're doing to my children's future, I hope you'll understand.

"Blake?"
"Yes, Dad?"
"Is greed good?"
"Of *course* not."

Blake is way too young to have seen either of Oliver Stone's R-rated attacks on modern capitalism, but she sure understands that the signature motto of Gordon Gekko in both *Wall Street* movies is not a sign of virtue. One of the real challenges for any parent—for anyone, really—when defending free-market capitalism is the Gekko problem: the perceived conflict between spending time helping others and spending time making money. Even the free market's biggest supporters find it easier to defend the prosperity it creates than the ways in which it does so. They're likely to concede that capitalism might put more money in our pockets but warn us to make sure it doesn't steal our souls at the same time.

The money-in-our-pockets phenomenon is not very controversial, though it's usually understated. The fact is that for the 98 percent or so of human civilization that occurred before Adam Smith wrote *The*

Wealth of Nations in 1776 (okay, some other stuff happened that year) the worldwide economy grew like pancake batter spreading out in a pan: It got a lot bigger—between 5000 BC and AD 1700, the world's population grew from about five million to five hundred million—but no higher. The amount produced by the average family (per capita GDP) barely moved during that entire 6,700-year period, which means not only that a weaver or mason or farmer living in Renaissance Europe didn't produce any more cloth or bricks or wheat than one living in ancient Egypt but also that the value of all that production was, in present-day terms, less than $900 a year per capita.

Today's worldwide per capita number, after two centuries of free-market capitalism, is more than $10,000 a year—and in the United States, more than $46,000.

You'd think that level of prosperity would be its own moral justification, since it measures not just how much people *produce* but also how much they can afford to *consume*; and increasing the average family's income by 1,000 percent also increases the number of years they live, how tall they grow, and how much food, health care, and education they can afford.

You'd think that. But you'd be wrong. The Obama family, and Progressives generally, make a strong (or, at least, a loud) case for the "helping" professions, as when the soon-to-be First Lady advised her listeners to stay out of corporate life and instead become teachers or nurses. For reasons that only they understand, the Progressives always *over*value a career spent providing people with charity and *under*value a life spent providing them with jobs.

Capitalism's critics are even older than the Progressive movement itself, though not by much; Karl Marx wrote *Capital* (*Das Kapital*) in 1867, only about twenty years before the start of the "Progressive Era." One hundred and fifty years later, the opinion pages are still blaming "unfettered" free markets (by which they mean, if my dictionary is correct, "free markets without leg irons" or "free markets that are free") for the Great Recession.

And even without those attacks, it's not easy to explain the value of free-market capitalism in a child's terms, since understanding the long-term importance of a growing economy requires a long-term view—something not exactly easy for a ten-year-old. Blake doesn't really have any way of comparing the abundance of products available today—cell phones, MP3 players, and personal computers, for example—to those available twenty years ago, much less two hundred. Moreover, Blake, like most kids (and all Progressives) tends to believe in fairness; and to her, and to Progressives, that means dividing the pie equally, not making it larger.[*]

From this sort of thinking—that the economy is a zero-sum game where every player's gain must be balanced by another player's loss—it's a short leap to the idea that anyone who has more than anyone else must be greedy—and, as we know, greed ain't good.

On the other hand, Blake *does* love animals . . .

"Blake?"

"Yes, Dad?

"You know how chimps groom each other?"

"Sure."

"What do you think would happen if a chimpanzee offered another one a piece of food and asked for help grooming as payment?"

"Depends on the chimp. If it was an average chimp, the second one would just take the food and run away."

"Actually, they almost always act as if 'one good turn deserves another.'"

"Why?"

"Because a chimp that just takes the food doesn't get offered anything next time."

"Kind of like a golden rule, right?"

---

* For information on how movies and television aimed at children reinforce this idea, see chapter 5.

....

This was actually what primatologist Frans de Waal described in a book called *Chimpanzee Politics*, but the even more interesting part is that chimps that regularly trade with one another are much more likely to cooperate on other matters, such as defending against an attack by a third chimp. Free trade, it seems, promotes cooperation as well.

And fairness, too. In looking for some examples of games I could use as a teaching tool for Blake, I came across one called Ultimatum, which has been used experimentally to test the ways that members of different cultures behave. Here's how the game is played: Participants pair off, with one player given a hundred points and the other none. The first player has to offer a portion of the points to the second; if the offer is accepted, the parties divide things that way; if not, no one gets anything. The way the rules are written, if second players accept *any* offer, they're still better off than if they decline it, since even an offer of ten points is more than nothing. But an offer of ten points is hardly ever accepted, since players sense it to be unfair.

Now here's the interesting part. A professor of psychology and economics named Joseph Henrich played the game with thousands of participants from fifteen different societies—hunter-gatherers, slash-and-burn farmers, nomadic herders, small-scale farmers, and so on. And what he found is that in societies with no or little trade—hunter-gatherer societies, for example—the average offer accepted is around twenty-five points (usually in the form of something less abstract than points, like food); but in societies with trade—and all industrial societies—the average number quickly approaches an even split. The freer and more familiar trade is, the fairer it tends to become.

The reason is that free markets depend on, and therefore promote, the virtue of trust. In fact, it's impossible to imagine free-market capitalism functioning without trust—and a lot of it. When I drop off my car for an oil change, I'm trusting that it will still be there when I return, and the mechanic who did the work is trusting that I'll pay for it. And that the credit card I use to pay will eventually transfer money into a different account. The credit-card company, of course, is trusting me to pay the bill at the end of the month. In societies without trade, no one *needs* to trust anyone else; in societies without freedom, no one is *able* to trust anyone else (see Soviet Union, and North Korea).

There are, in fact, a lot of virtues promoted by free markets, including diligence, hard work, and promptness (Adam Smith himself, in his *Lectures on Jurisprudence*, wrote, "When the greater part of people are merchants, they always bring probity and punctuality into fashion, and these are the principal virtues of commercial nations"). Free markets even promote the highest sort of morality: Our church teaches that the three theological virtues are faith, hope, and charity; free markets depend on the first two and make the third possible.

Free markets especially promote hope in the future, without which no new business would *ever* be started. Free-market societies are, by far, the best ones for dreamers and visionaries. And needless to say, for our children. Their futures depend on the number of choices they will have; free markets create more choices for more people, and those progressive slot machines—the idea that a nation's elites have the best idea how to allocate wealth and distribute income—reduce those choices. Whether the machines have been operated by Soviet commissars or social democrats, the result has differed only in degree.

And if that's not immoral, then I don't know what is.

CHAPTER 2

February 2009: The ABCs of the Free Market

In February 2009, when you couldn't turn on the TV without hearing someone talk about "bailouts" or "derivatives" or "stimulus packages" (usually without any idea what they were talking about), I asked Blake to write down any words or phrases that seemed to puzzle her—or, at least, to ask me to explain them.

Rereading those explanations months later, I can see that I might have allowed myself a small amount of opinionated commentary. Okay, a lot of opinionated commentary.

Advertising. Noun. Communication intended to persuade someone to take an action, where the persuader doesn't know the object of the communication.

Progressives hate advertising, at least whenever it's used to sell them something they don't approve of. This is even true in the media business itself, which would hardly exist without advertising dollars. Blake doesn't care for much of it herself and is unable to figure out why most of the commercials during *SpongeBob SquarePants* are promoting other Nickelodeon shows (she does make an exception for those times when an ad is more entertaining than whatever it is interrupting, as with the average Super Bowl). The three big objections to advertising are its constant presence, the belief that it misleads people into spending money on things they don't need (or, occasionally, voting for candidates they don't "really" support), and the cost it adds to the products and services they buy. I admit to sharing the first objection, even though a big chunk of every dollar I get paid is directly traceable to an advertisement; I knew we'd passed some sort of threshold when I saw that the plastic bins used to pass through airport security now included print ads. But the other two, like most Progressive beliefs, shrivel on close examination.

The idea that ads get people to do things they don't really want to do is really just another version of the idea that most people need to be told what they *should* want: a core Progressive notion. This is both insulting and just plain wrong: Almost all advertising is intended not to persuade people to buy beer or cars or a new-and-improved laundry detergent but to persuade them to buy one beer/car/detergent rather than another. To the degree that a rich economy offers consumers choices, there will be some sort of advertising intended to inform those choices. Even the idea that we need an entire body of law intended to regulate advertising is pretty hard to demonstrate. In fact, as Jeffrey Miron of Harvard University and the Cato Institute points out, a good case can be made that too much reliance on regulation makes people careless; if you really believed that everything you see is neither false or misleading, you are "way too gullible."

Even dumber is the idea that advertising results in an increase in the costs of goods and services and is therefore a drain on the economy. In 1922, when the U.S. gross domestic product was $73.4 billion, total advertising expenditures were $2.2 billion, or about 3 percent. In 2008, advertising had ballooned to a little less than $278 billion . . . or 2 percent of a $14 trillion economy. In short, it's a lot likelier that advertising is *responsible* for the incredible success story that is the U.S. economy than that it is some sort of hindrance to it.

Bailout. Noun. A way for taxpayers to pay off the debts of bankrupt companies without all the fuss and bother of a **bankruptcy**.

Bank. Noun. A financial middleman that accepts deposits (on which it typically pays **interest**) and pays and collects money promised against those deposits.

Ten-year-olds tend to have a pretty concrete view of the world, and to Blake, a bank is a building with a vault full of money. This is understandable: The bank on her corner is just a bigger version of the piggy bank in her bedroom. Explaining how this can be a *business* requires that the explainer—I—go back to first principles.

The only truly basic business for a bank is to collect money and guarantee the payments that its depositors make against that money. For hundreds if not thousands of years, bankers—the term "bank" comes from a word for the table on which money was accepted and exchanged; Blake's notion that a bank is a *place* isn't so far off—made their profit by charging their depositors for the service. It wasn't until sometime during the Middle Ages (probably) that some enterprising competitor came up with the idea that a better way to make money was to use the depositor's money to make loans and investments. There was so much money to be made with the depositor's money, in fact, that banks starting paying depositors for the privilege: paying interest for deposits and charging interest for loans.

Which brings us to the modern version of banking—and the peculiar modern problem that it presents to a free market. Banks obviously offer some pretty valuable functions in a free capitalist economy; without them, there's no way to borrow money to invest in business. However, since most people still want the bank to behave like Blake's piggy bank—to have their money on hand whenever they want it—the government regulates banking in a number of ways, some good (or at least not too bad) and others, well, not.

"Dad?"

"Yes, Blake?"

"Do you remember those silver dollars Mommy had? Where are they?"

"They're in the safety deposit box at the bank."

"Is that where all our money is?"

"Not exactly . . ."

The scariest thing about banks is that while everyone's money *can't* be paid out at once (since most of it has been lent or otherwise invested), everyone has to believe that they can get *theirs*. When they stop believing this and try to take their money out, panic sets in, since no one wants to be the last one in that particular line.

Enter regulators. Banks are required to keep a percentage of their total obligations on hand to pay their depositors, and the federal government guarantees deposits of up to $250,000. More recently, big banks have been given what is essentially a guarantee that no matter how reckless they are in the way they lend or invest their depositors' money, the federal government will absorb the risk—and as happens with all laws and policies intended to reduce the costs of risky behavior, the new regulations actually increased their frequency.

The Progressive response to yet another failure of regulation is, as usual, more regulations. Regulations that will forbid banks from trading on their own account, or trading **derivatives** at all. The idea here is that no bank that is "too big to fail" should be allowed to engage in practices that are going put it at risk of failure, with the costs of that failure borne by the taxpayer.

Deciding how big is too big is something that Progressive legislators and regulators practically salivate about. However, since the underlying logic of *all* banking regulation is to preserve depositors' access to their money—to make sure Blake can get those silver dollars back—there is actually a better, free-market solution, to that particular problem. Instead of worrying about the *kinds* of businesses that banks have, or about how *big* they are, we could simply require that they have enough money on hand to meet their obligations. If you fix capital requirements, you don't need to worry about being too big too fail, or derivatives trading, or any kind of trading at all. Are there costs to this particular free-market solution? Sure, but they are definitely less than the trillions of dollars that bailing out the current system is likely to cost.

Bankruptcy. Noun. The legal recognition that a debtor is unable to pay its creditors. Bankruptcy may be initiated by either a creditor or debtor but in practical terms is generally a voluntary act taken by a debtor to end pursuit by creditors. In the United States, bankruptcy can be a temporary protection while a debtor negotiates repayment and reorganizes. Or it can be the complete surrender of assets to a judge, who parcels them out to creditors.

Ask Blake what she thinks of when she hears the word "bankrupt," and she'll tell you that that's what happens to a player in Monopoly who has no money. Ask her what she thinks of when she hears the word "bailout," and she'll just look confused.

She's not the only one.

The reason generally offered up in support of the dozens of different bailout programs intended to blunt the collapse of 2008 was that bankruptcy for America's big financial institutions (well, most of them, anyway—see Lehman Brothers) would be too dangerous. But when a bank goes bankrupt, it doesn't vanish (though its shareholders may wish they could). Instead, someone takes over the assets and a bankruptcy judge resolves claims and sells off what's left. Someone buys them—a company that *didn't* do the things that caused the first one to go bankrupt in the first place.

Cap and trade. Noun. The so-called market-based method for reducing the amount of CO_2 emitted into the atmosphere by businesses. The "cap" is the amount of CO_2 each company is permitted, set by either government committee or auction; the "trade" refers to the way in which companies that need more permits can purchase them from companies that need fewer, thus setting a market price for emissions.

Whenever anyone starts moaning about the size of their (or my) "carbon footprint," I'm prone to ask them whether they mean the dirty lumps of coal left in bad kids' Christmas stockings or the carbon dioxide that is the end product of cellular respiration and the raw material for photosynthesis, which is to say, life on earth? Changing "CO_2" to "carbon" would make my old chemistry professors pretty testy, but no one can deny its PR value.

And it needs every bit of that value. I freely admit that I'm skeptical about many aspects of global climate change, but I also have to admit that Blake doesn't always share my skepticism. Her environmentalism is one of her defining characteristics, and she rarely meets a plan for saving the planet without falling in love with it. And you might think that a free-market zealot like me would love the idea of letting the marketplace set a price for CO_2. Or even carbon.

But there's a problem with cap and trade: There is no *real* market for CO_2 emissions, which is why the government has to make one. And whenever governments try to do what markets do, which is essentially allocate resources efficiently through pricing, they stink. Just do the numbers: Even if you buy the prediction by the UN's Intergovernmental Panel on Climate Change of a worldwide temperature increase of 2.8 degrees Celsius by 2100, you also have to accept its estimate that an increase of 4 degrees Celsius would result in a reduction in worldwide economic output of around 3 percent (and if this sounds a little less dire than Al Gore wants you to believe, see the PR comment above). If the cap-and-trade system currently proposed by the U.S. House of Representatives were to be fully implemented, however, the temperature increase would be only one-tenth of one degree Celsius less than it would be if the system weren't implemented. The economic benefit to the United States of such a reduction is tiny: one-fortieth of 1 percent of GDP. But the cost is 0.08 percent of GDP: at least ten times greater. Progressives are notoriously bad at arithmetic, but this is ridiculous.

Capitalism. Noun. A system in which a society's productive resources are privately owned and freely traded.

"Blake?"

"Yes, Dad?"

"Have you ever heard the word 'capital'"?

"The capital of the United States is Washington DC. And the state capitol is in Trenton. We went there on a field trip."

"Trenton?"

"That's the state capital, isn't it?"

It's probably too much to blame public education for preferring field trips to teaching basic economics. Most people have only a pretty sketchy idea about the basics of capitalism, partly because, in America at least, they don't really have anything to compare it with. The systems that preceded the idea that the best engine for economic growth (actually, the *only* engine for economic growth) was to allow capital goods—the land, factories, and patents that are used to make the goods people actually use: consumer goods—to be privately owned are long gone. The traditional systems of feudalism and mercantilism were actually intuitively pretty appealing for thousands of years because people thought all wealth was, finally, precious metal or land, and as a result, also thought that the total amount of it was finite.

Which, come to think of it, is the same argument used by Progressives to explain their eagerness to redistribute wealth from haves to have-nots.

CDO. Noun. Abbreviation for collateralized debt obligation. An investment whose value is based on a package of other fixed-income mortgages, corporate bonds, and mortgage-backed securities, whose complicated nature has been blamed for much of the crisis of 2008. CDO risks and prices are calculated using a mathematical technique known as cupola modeling, a multivariate joint distribution defined on the n-dimensional unit cube $[0,1]_n$ such that every marginal distribution is uniform on the interval $[0,1]$.

I don't understand it either.

CEO. Noun. Abbreviation for chief executive officer, the highest-ranking manager in a corporation, agency, or organization, who reports to the institution's board of directors. The Boss.

In 2009, the median CEO salary at America's five hundred largest corporations was about $8 million. This, we are told by Progressives, is a sign of the worst excesses of capitalism: CEOs taking home more than three hundred times what the average worker does, up from forty times that number thirty years ago. This is, like most such arguments, half information taken out of context, seasoned with a lot of envy.

The reaction to these more-than-generous incomes is pretty overheated. America's top five hundred CEOs earn more than Major League Baseball's 750 players and the four hundred (or so) members of NBA teams *combined*, and they don't offer nearly as much entertainment in return. However, there is less here than meets the eye. More than half of CEO compensation is in the form of stock and stock options, which means that the biggest reason they're paid so much is that the companies they manage have increased in value, which is a bargain that most shareholders probably applaud. It's also worth remembering that in 2009 the companies they manage generated more than $5 *trillion* in revenues, and their total pay is barely a rounding error.

This doesn't, of course, mean that every CEO is worth what he or she is paid. Every year, some prove that they are clearly not up to the job, or even able to stay on the right side of the law. And it seems possible that lots of companies could get the job done just as well by someone willing to work for less (though I wouldn't like to be the one to explain the decision to save a few million bucks to the board of directors of a hundred-billion-dollar company). But it does mean that attempts to legislate limits on CEO pay have about as much impact on a large company's efficiency as removing the embossing from business cards, no matter how much better it makes everyone feel.

Competition. Noun. In economics, the contest between individuals and companies to sell more goods and services.

Blake's feel for the rhythms of business may be a little erratic, but she understands competition. And she especially understands that winning—a race, a tennis match, a music competition—is a whole lot better than losing. The reason that competition is one of the basic principles of free-market economics starts from the same impulse but affects a lot more than a ten-year-old's self-esteem.

Adam Smith, the granddaddy of all free-market thinkers, was also the first to draw the link between free competition and increasing prosperity, pointing out that competition is the engine that allocates resources to their highest-valued use: If any business is good for the public, Smith wrote, "the freer and more general the competition, it will always be the more so." This has been taught to generations of introductory-economics students as the notion of *perfect competition*, which includes a number of, well, unlikely characteristics. For a business to qualify as perfectly competitive, it needs an infinite number of sellers (and consumers), no barriers to anyone wanting to enter the business, and no transaction or information costs—that is, when I want to shop for a widget, I can compare all the widgets instantaneously without stirring from my chair. In such a consumer's Garden of Eden, all prices for widgets will eventually be only a tiny bit higher than the cost of making them.

To a lot of people the nonexistence of such perfectly competitive markets outside of introductory economics textbooks means that (a) free markets don't really work as well as described; and (b) governments have to intervene to make sure that **monopolies** don't grow where competition used to exist. Both ideas are favorites of Progressives. And both (surprise!) are wrong.

While perfect competition makes for neat equations, the fact is that even imperfect competition is pretty good. In fact, a little bit of competition is better than none, more competition is better than a little, and a lot of competition is better still. Monopolies (see below; actually businesses with some monopoly pricing power) will always emerge, as one firm or individual takes advantage of a superior idea or just plain luck. But in a free market, they don't last, as other firms, attracted by the profits that a monopolist earns, enter the business. The only monopoly pricing power that lasts, in fact, is the sort that is *created* by the government. As always, the Progressives have it exactly backward: Competition doesn't need government help; it generally only suffers from it.

Consumption. Noun. The purchase of goods and services by end users, i.e., consumers, rather than businesses or government.

You'd think that economics could agree on a definition of consumption, which is, after all, their primary subject. You'd be wrong. In addition to the definition above, a lot of economists (and policy makers) measure consumption as every economic transaction that *isn't* either design, production, or selling. **John Maynard Keynes**, along with his many other dubious contributions, defined it as all income that isn't saved or invested, which leads to the notion that if you borrow money and then spend it, you've increased consumption without increasing income. Come to think of it, this explains how the national **debt** got to be so large that it now has fourteen digits.

Eventually, *consumption* of goods and services and *production* of goods and services have to even out. However, eventually can be a long time, which is why both households and governments frequently find themselves so far behind the eight ball. Some economists argue that the best way to improve things is to tax consumption rather than income, but the governments that listen to them inevitably end up taxing both.

Creative destruction. Compound noun. The principle that, in a free market, innovation creates new businesses at the expense of old.

The idea that capitalist economies grow by killing off existing enterprises was not original to the Austrian economist Joseph Schumpeter, who named it the "perennial gale of creative destruction" in 1942. A century earlier, Karl Marx, of all people, was writing about the eternally disruptive nature of capitalism—a nature that didn't bother Marx all that much but sure gives fits to a lot of other folks: not just Progressives who reflexively think that any sort of economic pain is a sign of market failure but also conservatives whose real allegiance is to a society organized along the most traditional lines.

It isn't a very happy thought for your typical ten-year-old, either.

"It's just not fair."

"What isn't fair, Blake?"

"The candy store, Dad."

"What about the candy store?"

"It's closing, and that means that no one is going to sell those good vanilla-and-chocolate lollipops anymore."

It's one thing that Blake has in common with the most reactionary *and* the most collectivist impulses: the desire to keep the forces of change at bay. The belief in some sort of "endangered businesses act" is understandable, at least for someone Blake's age. Free market capitalism *has* been an unmatched engine of prosperity for centuries, but that doesn't mean that it delivered that prosperity without any suffering along the way: Jobs vanish, companies and even entire industries disappear, and it speaks well for Blake's compassion that she isn't exactly cheering for it, even when it's only a corner candy store.

When that compassion turns into policies that protect jobs and industries that aren't going to survive on their own, however, the cost is economic decline. America had more than 100,000 harness makers in 1900, and more than 200,000 blacksmiths. Twenty years later, the country was a *lot* richer, but that doesn't mean that a lot of formerly prosperous families weren't suffering. Schumpeter made an analogy to evolution by natural selection—he called new "species" of business "industrial mutations," in case anyone missed the point: Extinction was hard on the dinosaurs, but it was a godsend for the ancestors of all the mammals walking the earth today, including Blake.

Credit. Noun. The transfer of something valuable from one person or firm to another, when payment for it is delayed until a later date.

It's not very hard to figure out how a word from the Latin root meaning "to trust or believe" ended up meaning both the recognition of an actor's work in a movie or play and the amount of money a bank is willing to lend. Blake doesn't quite get it:

"Dad?"

"Yes, Blake?"

"How does a credit card work?"

"When you use a credit card to buy something, you still have to pay for what you bought, but you do it later, instead of right now."

"When I get extra credit for a project, is that later or right now?"

"There are lots of kinds of credit, Blake. What the two meanings have in common is acknowledging that something is owed."

"Like when my name is in a concert program, they call it a credit?"

"Exactly: You are owed some recognition for playing the guitar. When you get extra credit, that recognizes that you did more than you needed to on a test. And when you buy something on credit, you're recognizing that you owe the person you bought it from."

"Too many meanings, Dad."

Well, maybe. The credit that means buying today and paying tomorrow isn't really unique to a free market—lots of *unfree* markets happily accept its benefits—but it does depend on trust: trust that someone will pay what is owed. Which is a lot easier than the other essential aspect of credit, which is understanding that a dollar tomorrow is worth less than one today.

. . . .

"Blake, would you rather have a dollar right now, or tomorrow?

"Doesn't matter."

"How about a year from now?"

"Then I'd rather have it now."

"What if I gave you a choice of a buck today, or two bucks a year from now?"

"I'd rather have the money today."

"How about ten dollars?"

"Still rather have it now."

Blake's time value of money is a little steep. Eventually, though, even she will get the idea that if you make the cost of lending money too high, no one will borrow any. But you (or rather, your happy-go-lucky government) can also make the cost too low; when that happens, too many people borrow money, and not all of them will pay it back. "Trust or belief," indeed.

Debt. Noun. An obligation to pay, at a later date, for assets acquired in the present; future purchasing power.

There are those who think that the ability to discount is at the core of modern capitalism, and the huge variety of debt instruments reflect this. From the simplest bank loan (fixed amount of money repaid at fixed rate of interest over fixed amount of time) to letters of credit (maximum amount fixed, but interest paid only on the money actually used) to corporate and government bonds, inflation-indexed debt, mezzanine obligations, syndicated loans—the list is endless. As are the zeros on the end of the debt currently owed by the United States to various creditors: more than $8 trillion. (It also owes more than $4 trillion to itself, in the form of future Social Security and the like.)

Debt is not always bad. If the only things people and businesses could buy were things for which they had cash on hand, there'd be a lot fewer factories, apartment buildings, commercial airplanes, and so on. Borrowing money against the future money-generating potential of an asset is a much better allocation of resources than saving it by burying it in the backyard (putting it in the bank is just lending it to someone else). However, the potential for, shall we say, overshooting the mark, seems obvious, and—to Blake—it is:

"Do you know what's wrong with debt, Blake?"

"Well . . . you can start here [she places her hand about belt high], but before too long you're here [her hand moves to just below her chin], and pretty soon here [hand above head; drowning noises]."

Depression, Great. Noun. The worldwide economic collapse that began in the United States in 1929, spread around the world, and caused an unprecedented loss of wealth, income, and productivity for an entire decade, with unemployment between 25 percent and 30 percent, crop prices falling by more than half, deflation, completely frozen credit, and untold misery. For many decades, almost everyone seemed to agree that the Depression was the result of unregulated markets gone wild and that it was cured (or at least made less bad) by the policies and jobs programs of the New Deal. Today it is pretty respectable to argue that the Depression was the *result* of misguided governmental intervention (such as increasing tariffs) and that the impact of the New Deal was, at best, nothing—and that it was possibly even harmful.

The only good thing about the Great Depression is that it has made all other economic crises—including the current one—seem like a mild head cold.

Derivatives. Plural noun. Agreements or contracts whose value is determined by the price of something else.

Futures, swaps, options . . . All derivatives are financial instruments that have no underlying value (how can they?), but that doesn't mean they have no *market* value, though the mathematical formulas used to calculate those values make subatomic physics look easy (see **CDO**). There's nothing intrinsically wrong with allowing people to gamble on the change in value of a stock or a piece of real estate (usually, actually a package of mortgages on different sorts of real estate), and a good case can be made that allowing people to bet that the value of one investment might not increase—the term is "hedging"— actually allows investors to insure themselves against bad outcomes (which is what insurance is for) and even makes even more information about pricing available—and the more information about how people value things, the more efficient the market.

Even so, derivative investments are not for the faint of heart. The fact that (a) hundreds of billions are wagered daily on contracts whose value moves in the opposite direction from the underlying investment; (b) some trades are derived from things that have *no* underlying market, like hurricane activity; and (c) some derivative contracts are worth hundreds or thousands of times as much as the underlying investment to which they are tied, means that small problems can turn into gigantic ones in the blink of an eye.

Efficiency. Noun. In economics, the degree to which allocation of resources results in the maximum production of goods and services. A system is efficient* when markets are in equilibrium: enough supply and demand at every price point.

Since it is mathematically provable that a competitive market is also the most efficient, the kind of reflexive hostility to markets that are the hallmark of Progressivism requires either arguing that markets aren't competitive or defining true efficiency not as the *most* goods and services at the lowest cost but as a *socially desirable* amount. Progressives do this by arguing that **externalities** like air pollution or discrimination against women need to be counted in the price of everything. Everyone who makes this argument also argues that he knows what that price is.

Externalities. Noun. In an economic transaction, costs or benefits that aren't incorporated into the price.

---

* Sometimes called "Pareto efficient" or "Pareto optimal" for the Italian economist Vilfredo Pareto, who defined it as a situation where it is impossible to make someone better off without making someone else worse off. Kind of like free agency in baseball.

Anytime you hear someone talking about externalities, you are in the presence of Progressives, and you should count the silver before they leave.

Fair trade. Noun. The belief that certain agricultural commodities need a minimum price, without which trade is, presumably, unfair to the farmers who produce them. No one has yet figured out how to establish such a price, much less make sure that it actually enriches farmers rather than the bureaucrats who decide whether a particular price is "fair."*

Fiat money. Noun. Currency issued without any right to convert it to anything else.

Friedman, Milton. American economist (1912–2006) who was the twentieth century's most prominent and effective advocate of free-market capitalism. Awarded the Nobel Memorial Prize in Economic Sciences in 1976. Author of dozens of books and articles, including 1980's *Free to Choose*, written with his wife, Rose.

Milton Friedman casts a ridiculously large shadow over twentieth-century economics, in technical areas like consumer behavior and monetarism (the idea that the only really important economic responsibility of the government is to keep the supply of money growing at a constant rate), but wouldn't be worth mentioning in this book if he hadn't also been the most successful advocate for the free market since **Adam Smith**. In fact, he went a lot further, arguing, among other things, for abolishing virtually every governmental agency and even the requirement that doctors be licensed.

People love to do the old compare-and-contrast game with Friedman and **John Maynard Keynes**, but the real key to understanding the importance of both men is the **Great Depression**, which persuaded a whole lot of people that free markets had failed (sound familiar?). For decades, the Keynesian solution to the great unemployment of the 1930s had been for government to spur demand

---

* For more on fair trade, see chapter 8.

by spending money. Hidden in all of this was the germ of the worst Progressive myth: Since people don't know best how and when to spend their own money, government employees need to do so on their behalf.

Friedman wasn't having any of it. Almost single-handedly, he revived the idea that people *do* make the best decisions about their own wealth, that they "maximize utility" (which is usually defined as choosing the highest-valued alternative available) not just in the short term but over their entire lifetimes. If he hadn't done anything else, this would have secured his position as *the* great free-market thinker of the era.

GDP. Noun. Acronym for gross domestic product, the sum of all economic output in a single country or (less commonly) some smaller or larger political unit.

GDP is supposed to represent the market value of all goods and services that are made in a single year, but measuring something so complicated is, well, complicated. Economists and policy makers calculate GDP three different ways, each of which is supposed to add up to the same number and occasionally even does. The first one is a simple measure of the total output of every business, assembled by surveying; the second is the amount spent on that output;* and the third is the total value of all producers' incomes. Getting there means measuring national consumption, investment, government spending, exports, capital formation . . . You get the idea.

However the calculation is performed, the idea behind GDP is to measure a country's economic activity rather than its welfare or standard of living. This is, I guess, the reason that Progressives are so unhappy with it, and especially with the notion that more GDP is better than less GDP. It's so unsatisfactory for the stuff that *really* matters to the Progressive mind—things like environmental damage

---

* Because the "D" in GDP stands for "domestic" expenditure, calculations have to take out the value of imports and exports . . . not that you asked.

or sustainability or disparities between rich and poor—that inventing alternatives to GDP has become a growth industry all its own.

The Kingdom of Bhutan, for example, located north of India, has led the way in calculating something called GNH, gross national happiness, which surveys, among other things, how many antidepressants are prescribed annually (bad) or the percentage of voters participating in local democracy (good). Then there's the GPI, genuine progress indicator, a creation of the United Nations System of National Accounts, which records such measures as the loss of farmland or degree of noise pollution (both bad). Then there's the Happy Planet Index, which ranks countries on a scale of something called happy life years and places the Dominican Republic and Cuba far above Switzerland and Italy.

If these seem a little squishy to you, well, they do to me, too. GDP isn't a perfect measure of anything, but it has two pretty large virtues that make it superior to any of the competing measures—yes, even the Happy Planet Index.

The first of those virtues is that no one rigs GDP measurements so that a particular group's ideas about "the good life" are given extra points; though most of the games played with calculating living standards are intended to serve a Progressive agenda—happy life years include measures for (I swear) "Discrimination of Women," "Brotherhood," "Tolerance," and "Social Justice"—it would be just as dishonest to rank countries by the number of hours the average person spends in prayer.

The second virtue is that GDP—especially per capita GDP, which is the total of goods and services produced by the average person in a particular country—unlike its competitors, actually *is* correlated with pretty much every aspect of human welfare that we can measure, including life span, infant mortality, and literacy.

Oh, there's a third reason to like GDP as a measure of national economic performance: It makes Progressives apoplectic.

Gold. Noun. Chemical element Au, atomic number 79. Also the precious metal used to back currency anywhere that has used the gold standard.

"Dad?"

"Yes, Blake?"

"Why do all these commercials want to buy your gold?"

"Because they think they can make more money when they sell it."

"But isn't gold a *kind* of money?

"Not anymore."

"Didn't it used to be?"

Using a given sum of a precious metal as a way of calculating the economic value of a currency is thousands of years old. In its original form, the money in circulation actually *was* gold (or, more frequently, silver) but even paper currency, for most of its history, has been exchangeable for gold at a fixed price.

That all changed, like so much else, with the **Great Depression**. Through the first years of the Depression, the Federal Reserve still paid for dollars with gold, but after the banking panics of the era reminded every depositor that it might be a good idea to convert their bank deposits into something a bit shinier, demand exceeded supply, and in 1933, the United States announced that it would no longer agree to such exchanges.

This didn't mean that the United States, or anyone else, abandoned the gold standard; after World War II, most of the world's large economies agreed to fix their own currencies to the U.S. dollar, and the United States agreed to fix the price of gold at $35 an ounce. And so it stayed, until 1971, when President Richard Nixon announced that dollars would no longer equal a fixed amount of gold (and he didn't stop there, imposing a ninety-day freeze on all wages and prices in the United States), shocking the world's financial system and introducing the volatility that we've lived with ever since.

The volatility of the last forty years hasn't been a curse, but as blessings go, it is a pretty complicated one. Because once a dollar is unmoored from a given amount of gold—the term is "floating"—it starts to act like a share of stock, which means that its value is whatever a bunch of traders think is its future value. This kind of risk is hedged by **derivatives**, **CDO**s, and other complicated financial instruments, with a lot of potential for profit—and mischief.

On the other hand, returning to a gold standard, or something like it, isn't really all that attractive either. Though requiring the government to have a given amount of gold for all the money in circulation prevents **inflation** (by definition, you can't have more dollars around than you have gold) and reduces uncertainty, it also creates the risk of **deflation** whenever the economy grows faster than the gold supply. According to the U.S. Geologic Survey, the total amount of gold that has ever been mined is "only" about 142,000 metric tons, which, at a price of $1,200 an ounce—what it was trading for as of July 2010—would be a bit less than $5 trillion; and the Federal Reserve calculates that nearly $9 trillion is currently in circulation in the United States alone.

Some pretty sane economists—and a *whole* lot of libertarians—still think that it might be worthwhile to return to some kind of "hard" currency. I'm not one of them, though I'm sympathetic to anything that takes control of the economy out of the hands of a bunch of bureaucrats. It might be a more stable world if the dollar were tied to something like gold (though the argument that paper has no "intrinsic value" isn't very persuasive either; what's gold good for, anyway, other than filling teeth and making jewelry?), but I'll take my chances on letting the marketplace set the prices of most things, including the folding money in my pocket.

Hayek, Friedrich A. Political philosopher and economist (1899–

---

* Not as much as it sounds. This quantity of gold would be a cube about one hundred feet on a side.

1992) who made basic contributions to the study of free-market capitalism, price signals, and monetary theory. Author of, most famously, *The Road to Serfdom*. Winner of the Nobel Memorial Prize in Economic Sciences in 1974.

From the 1920s, when the Austrian-born Hayek was hired to work at the London School of Economics by Ludwig von Mises (another member of the free-market pantheon), until his death, he was collectivism's fiercest enemy. Part of his hostility to the enthusiasm for state control of the economy, which has been such a durable part of the European mind-set, was Hayek's belief that it led directly to totalitarianism, which, given the history of Europe since the 1930s, is supported by an awful lot of evidence.

But he didn't just oppose it on political grounds. Collective decisions about economic issues require some kind of overall authority, and while they do a lousy job, they have always had a lot of appeal to Progressives. And some, but by no means all, ten-year-olds.

"Blake?"

"Yes, Dad?"

"When you have a bake sale at school, who decides that the brownies should be fifty cents apiece?"

"The person who made the brownies, I guess."

"If you sold all the brownies, and people asked for more, does that mean that fifty cents was the right price?"

"I guess."

"And if you didn't sell any?"

"Maybe they liked chocolate cookies more."

"Would you think the person might have picked the wrong price?"

Blake gave me a wordless what-a-stupid-question look. "Of course."

"Would you still want the person to set the price next time?"

"Nope. I'd want to set the price myself."

. . . .

The idea that efficient exchange demands price signals seems pretty obvious, but there's still a ten-year-old inside most people who doesn't trust a system without someone running it. Hayek's great insight was that even without anyone at the controls, a price-signaling system (as we'll see in chapter 4, he called it "catallaxy," though no one else does) actually spontaneously organizes itself.

Of course, such a system depends on private property, freely traded, which is one reason that he was one of Ronald Reagan's favorite economists.

Higgs effect. Noun. Sometimes known as the Higgs ratchet effect. The phenomenon that transforms temporary economic crises into permanent government involvement in the economy, to no good effect.

The experience described by libertarian economist Robert Higgs in his 1987 book *Crisis and Leviathan* was really just the latest in a series of cautionary tales that dates back to James Madison, who warned against "the old trick of turning every contingency into a resource for accumulating force in government." The "ratchet" of his effect refers to the reliable fact that, even though every crisis—the Great Depression or the recession of 2008—eventually ends, and the enthusiasm for state intervention may recede, it never returns to the level it occupied before the crisis. Consider, for example, the Export-Import Bank of the United States, which was created in 1934 to combat the worst effects of the Great Depression by providing loan guarantees to banks that agreed to lend to buyers of American exports.

Partly because it costs the American taxpayer nothing, covering its costs by charging fees to foreign borrowers, the Ex-Im Bank has a lot of supporters. None of them is bigger than the aircraft manufacturer Boeing, which accounted for 40 percent of Ex-Im Bank's business in 2009. This is not a misprint; a government agency established to fight an economic crisis seventy-five years ago now exists in large part as an ongoing subsidy for a single company. The distortions of this sort of cronyism are hard to miss: by some estimates, an oversupply of nearly 10 percent in commercial airplanes. (This is nothing compared to the record of Freddie Mac and Fannie Mae; see chapter 10). The only certain thing about emergencies is that, over time, every one of them increases government involvement in the economy.

For people who actually think government knows best—you know, the people who never want to "waste" a crisis—this is a good thing. For free markets, however, it's like increasing Blake's allowance; once we give her a raise, we find it next to impossible to take it back.

Income tax. Noun. The part of the earnings of people and businesses that are levied (this is another word for "taken") by local, state, and national governments.

Income taxes can be *flat*—where everyone pays the same percentage of their income—*progressive*, where the more you earn the higher the percentage you pay, or *regressive*, where the more you earn the lower the percentage you pay. This sounds simple, but it isn't. In fact, the federal law that defines what income can be taxed and at what rates is now more than 55,000 pages long. This is not a misprint. Once upon a time, before the tax code crossed the four-million-word mark, the government assumed that people owned 100 percent of their income, and levied—okay, took—what was needed to run itself. Recently, we've started assuming that the government owns 100 percent of your income and, after it gets done running itself, allows you to keep the part left over. The two definitions are equal mathematically, but not in any other way. The notion that all income begins as a possession of the government is why some people call activity that *isn't* taxed a "tax subsidy." This is like one kid stealing some of another kid's candy and calling the rest a "dessert subsidy."

There is a whole lot more justification for a *negative income tax*, a favorite of **Milton Friedman**, in which people earning less than a specified amount receive a subsidy, than for a positive one. Taking care of the poor by simply giving them money is definitely better than the constellation of antipoverty programs currently littering federal and state government. Two reasons: First, it returns some level of personal responsibility to people who are, either through bad luck or just a lack of effort, unable to support themselves. Second, it eliminates thousands of useless jobs for people who supervise, plan, evaluate, and manage anti-poverty programs, leaving everything to the (relatively) simple Internal Revenue Service. Of course, this may have the effect of making all those social workers, consultants, and community organizers eligible for the negative income tax themselves . . .

Inflation and **deflation.** Nouns. Inflation is an increase in the price of a good or service over time; deflation is a decrease. Popularly, the terms are used to describe increases and decreases in the overall package of goods and services purchased by a typical family: a rise or fall in the Consumer Price Index.

Inflation—which **Milton Friedman** called "taxation without legislation"—basically comes in two flavors: an increase in the amount of money in circulation (or, back in the days when **gold** and silver coins were used as money, the addition of cheaper, or base, metal, which is where the term "debasement" of the currency comes from) or just an overall increase in prices. Generally, the first definition is reserved for something that economists call "monetary inflation."

The other sort of inflation (or deflation) is calculated in a dizzying number of ways, but in general the price of a package of goods and services on one date is compared with the same package a year later to come up with an annual inflation rate. There are huge problems with this over any really long period of time, since the "package" itself changes (even the wealthiest family today spends a lot more on, for example, Internet service and a lot less on servants than it did fifty years ago), and even components of the package aren't really comparable: A gallon of gasoline costs five times as much as it did when I got my first driver's license, but the car I fill up today gets twice as many miles per gallon.

Inflation doesn't "tax" everyone the same way. People who borrow money in an inflationary economy tend to do pretty well, since they repay their loans with money that is worth a lot less than it was the day they borrowed it; lenders, on the other hand, get burned. The belief that house prices would continue to inflate more rapidly than the economy at large persuaded millions of borrowers *and* lenders to buy property at very high prices, convinced that they could sell it at an even higher price (this is sometimes known as the "greater fool" phenomenon). However, since deflation is usually a sign of enormous financial stress (and *hyper*inflation—when the value of currency can fall so far that you need to carry banknotes to the grocery store in a wheelbarrow—is even worse), it's generally a good idea to have some inflation.

However, the idea that inflation is the price for full employment, so beloved of Progressives and followers of **Keynes**, died during the 1970s, when the world was able simultaneously to have high levels of both inflation and unemployment, forever after known as "stagflation."

Innovation. Noun. The successful application of a new idea.

One of the biggest errors made by the first generation of economists, such as **Adam Smith**, David Ricardo, and others, was the belief that free markets would eventually drive profits down to zero and wages to subsistence level, as competition eliminated the ability of both producers and workers to charge more than their most aggressive competitor; the technical term is the "disappearance of monopoly pricing power."

Well, profits haven't vanished, and average wages have increased several hundredfold since Smith's day. The reason, in a nutshell, is innovation—and it is just as much a part of the free market as the "invisible hand." The new ideas that are the raw material of innovation have been appearing at an ever-increasing rate ever since the law started recognizing a property right not just in tangible things such as land and gold but in intangible things such as inventions and copyrights. Steam engines, telephones, automobiles, and computers aren't just responsible for a big chunk of the wealth of the modern world; they also create a world different enough from the perfect competition envisioned by classical economists that firms can enjoy—temporarily—enough monopoly pricing power that they can both generate big profits (Apple's iPhone, anyone?) and pay very high wages, indeed.

And even if the power is temporary, who cares? That's really what **creative destruction** is all about. Societies that recognize a property right in ideas never run short of them, or of the innovation needed to make them successful.

Interest. Noun. The price paid for borrowing anything, usually money; by extension, the amount earned on a deposit account that is used by someone else as borrowed money. The difference between the amount paid on deposits and that earned by lending is the bulk of a bank's **profit**.

As mentioned above (in the entry for **credit**), Blake's idea of a reasonable interest rate is a little high, but everyone has a different view of what is a worthwhile rate. Once upon a time, government-insured certificates of deposit in banks were paying more than 15 percent interest; in 2010 that number has been less than 2 percent. The amount of return expected from lending money, either directly to borrowers or indirectly through bank deposits, is a function of the alternatives foregone. When stocks are booming, banks need to pay high interest rates to entice investors to take their money out of the market and put it in the bank. So do governments and businesses when they issue bonds that also pay a fixed rate of interest. One of the most reliable signs of trouble is when the interest rate paid on the safest imaginable investments is extremely low; in 1933, the worst year of the Depression, U.S. Treasury bills were paying a rate of 0.14 percent annually.

Keynes, John Maynard. British economist (1883–1946) and architect of the Bretton Woods 1944 system of fixed exchange rates among nations, pegged to the U.S. dollar. Author of numerous books and articles, most notably the 1936 *General Theory of Employment, Interest, and Money*, which introduced the set of concepts known as "Keynesianism" to the world.

Like everyone who lived through the **Great Depression**, Keynes was changed forever by it. Unlike most everyone else, he thought he had found a solution to it (or at least its frighteningly high unemployment rate) in the economic philosophy that became known as Keynesianism, whose most basic idea was that full employment demands government expenditures. Keynes was no Marxist, much less a socialist, but the source of his ideas still seems to be a kind of scorn for the idea that people can make economically rational decisions; "animal spirits," in his words, drive most business decisions and are not only disreputable but also unreliable.

For Progressives in search of a theory to back up their instinct that bureaucrats know best, this has been a godsend. Reviewing **Hayek**'s *Road to Serfdom* (which he called "a grand book"), Keynes wrote, "What we want is not no planning, or even less planning; indeed I should say we almost certainly want more."

Krugman, Paul. American economist (1953–), professor at Princeton University and the London School of Economics and columnist for the *New York Times*. Winner of the 2008 Nobel Memorial Prize in Economic Sciences.

There are at least two different Paul Krugmans. One is a fairly wonky college professor who has specialized in the intricacies of international trade, written eloquently on the virtues of free trade, and attacked government intervention in the economy, including rent control, minimum-wage laws, farm subsidies, and "strategic industry" investment. The other one isn't.

The one who isn't has written a dozen books and more than eight hundred columns for the *New York Times* attacking conservatives in every walk of life. In these books and columns, he typically supports more governmental intervention in the economy (no matter how big the intervention, as with the $700 billion Troubled Asset Relief Program of 2008 and the multitrillion-dollar stimulus programs of 2009 and 2010, it never seems to be enough), policies to promote income equality even at the cost of income growth, and anything that lays the evils of the world at the feet of the Republican Party generally and George W. Bush specifically. This Krugman is an avowed welfare-state supporter whose worst collectivist instincts have been unleashed by his position at the *New York Times* (which shouldn't, after all, surprise anyone) to the point that his former support for open immigration and free trade has become so watered down that it is unrecognizable. Like most Progressives, Krugman-the-columnist is far happier spending time thinking how to divide the economic pie fairly than thinking how to make it larger.

Leverage. Noun. The amount by which gains and losses may be multiplied in any transaction; verb (informal). The technique of multiplying gains and losses. Typical forms of leverage include investing with borrowed money and investing in **derivatives**. (Note: In corporate accounting, leverage is a measure of the relationship between revenues and net income—that is, how much difference a percentage-point increase in sales makes in a company's **profit.**)

The key measure of a banking system's health—or vulnerability—is the amount of leverage represented by the difference between its worst-case obligations and its best-case assets. See **Risk.**

Monopoly. Noun. (Blake: "This is not the board game.") A business in which a single firm or individual is the only seller of a particular good or service; from the Greek *monos*, or "one," and *polein*, or "seller." A "monopsony" is a business with a single buyer; an "oligopoly" (or "oligopsony") is one with only a few buyers or sellers. Absolute monopolies are virtually nonexistent, but the term "monopoly pricing power" is used to describe the freedom with which some businesses can set prices for their products.

The real reason that governments have laws to limit monopolies is the theory that monopolies can charge whatever they want for their product or service. However, the ability to charge a lot—that "monopoly pricing power"—is actually pretty limited. In a free market, when a company is so dominant that its profits head toward the stratosphere, it inevitably attracts a competitor with an eye on those profits. In fact, the *only* time this doesn't happen is when—you guessed it—the government itself discourages, or even forbids, competition. There may be times when this isn't too bad (once upon a time, AT&T owned a government-granted monopoly on phone service, under the theory that nobody wanted a competition for building the most telephone poles down every street), but it is always to be regarded with skepticism.

Price. Noun. The payment made by one person to another in return for goods or services.

Prices don't have to be made in terms of money; barter, for example, can still serve to set a price for any particular exchange. Nor does a price have to be fixed. Auctions set prices based on the highest value that can be charged. Prices can be expressed as "nominal" (dollars and cents) or "real" (as compared to another good or service). They can be stated as the balance point between the marginal utility and the marginal cost of a particular object—the benefit or cost of the last one bought or sold.

However, in a free market, the real significance of price is that it is the way in which sellers tell buyers how much they want of something. The immense power of price signals, all by themselves, to "direct" business decisions, is the reason that free markets are both better organized and far more productive than controlled ones.

Profit. Noun. An increase in wealth from any productive pursuit or investment.

You might think that "profit" is a pretty simple thing to define, whether you're running General Electric or a corner lemonade stand: revenue minus costs. But nothing is simple once economists get hold of it. "Cost," for example, isn't just the five dollars you paid for the lemons and sugar at the supermarket; it's also the value of something else you might otherwise have done with the same five bucks. In fact, it's the value of the *most* valuable thing you might have done, which is what economists call your "opportunity cost."

Which is why, when Blake and Scott assemble the ingredients for that hypothetical lemonade stand, their "normal profit" is not just the cost of the lemonade mix (the water, table, sign, and chairs aren't free, exactly, but are positive **externalities**) but the value they put on spending that money—and their time—on something else.

Regulation and **deregulation.** Nouns. Regulation is the process of controlling behavior, usually economic behavior, by rules, or any individual rule designed to do so. Deregulation is the elimination of one or more such rules.

Though regulation can be voluntary (as when an association tries to get its members to abide by a particular behavior), the term usually refers to the kind of rules that have the force of law—the regulations imposed by government to ensure a particular outcome that wouldn't happen in an unregulated free market.

Even a hard-core libertarian recognizes the need for *some* government regulation, if only to enforce contract laws. But as always with any government activity, anything worth doing is, soon enough, worth overdoing, and the various levels of government in the United States currently regulate construction permits, professional licenses (for everyone from surgeons to cosmetologists), advertising, the nutritional components of food, and the prices paid for literally thousands of commodities.

While there is a rationalization for every one of these regulations—generally some amorphous conception of the "public good," as when the City of New York proposed limiting the amount of salt in restaurant food—there are two profound free-market objections to regulation in general: First, governments are very bad at calculating the costs and benefits of regulation—not surprising, since the cost of regulation is almost entirely borne by businesses. This is why multimillion-dollar dams are hostage to the habitat of a single population of fish or birds, why the Food and Drug Administration tries to ban food colorings with a risk of one death in ten *billion*, and why **cap-and-trade** legislation is projected to cost about ten times as much as the benefit it might realize.

But there's another reason for libertarians—for anyone, really—to be suspicious of regulation, and that's the unavoidable fact that politicians make decisions, well, politically (see Nowhere, Bridges to). Regulation may be necessary—but it should always be regarded as a necessary evil.

Risk. Noun. The probability that a future event will diverge from its expected value; the chance of a particular event occurring multiplied by its monetary (or other) cost or benefit.

It's a pretty short jump from the idea that people are irrational about risk (especially financial risk) to the idea that they need to be protected from it.

"Blake, I have ten boxes here. One of them has a dollar bill inside." I move it to the left side of the table. "One of the other nine has a ten-dollar bill in it." I move the other nine to the right. "Which one do you want?"

Blake picks one of the nine boxes on the right.

"What if there were twenty boxes on the right, and one of them had a ten-dollar bill in it?

She still picks one of the boxes on the right. Blake likes long shots.

Though risk is, technically, just as much a measure of positive uncertainty as negative, the popular understanding is overwhelmingly about the likelihood that bad things might occur; when people talk about the risk of global climate change, they aren't referring to the possibility that Siberia might become as fertile as California's Central Valley (though they would if they had a proper understanding of risk).

45

A good case can be made that the most important difference between today's economies and yesterday's is the degree to which we have developed tools to measure, and manage, risk rather than to fear it. This difference in the understanding of risk is one of the most dramatic differences between Progressives and free-market advocates. When a welfare state tries to remove the dangers of bad economic outcomes—and, to be fair, when businesses ask to be rescued by government from either bad luck or their own ineptitude—they are trying to *eliminate* the element of risk; when entrepreneurs start new businesses, they are doing their best to *manage* it. It's no accident that "risk" is derived from an Italian word, *risicare*, meaning "to dare." Blake's attraction to the big payoff, even in the face of poor odds, is classic entrepreneurial behavior. John Nye, an economist at George Mason University, has made a career proving that *irrational* choices—what he calls "lucky fools"—are the foundation of real economic growth.

Scarcity. Noun. Insufficiency or shortage of supply.

One of the most important lessons Penelope and I try to teach Blake and Scott is that they will always want more stuff—desserts, video games, musical instruments—than there is stuff available, which means that they have to choose. This is also the core of all economics, free market or otherwise: the idea that people always want more of things of which there are, at any moment, a finite amount.

Scarcity is what gives things value, but the way it does so isn't all that obvious. The first free-market economists thought that people valued things based on what it cost them—in pain or effort—to acquire. The bigger the nuisance you were willing to suffer, the more you valued whatever you were suffering for. Since the 1930s or so, value from scarcity has been generally defined (by a group of economists from Vienna, the so-called Austrian School, led by **Friedrich Hayek**) as an opportunity cost: not the effort or pain required but the "highest-valued alternative foregone."

Not, you may think, the easiest concept to communicate to a ten-year-old.

"Blake?"

"Yes, Dad?

"What is the value of that new guitar you've been eyeing?"

"You mean, what does it cost?"

"Sort of. The value is what you're *willing* to pay for it, not what someone *wants* you to pay for it—though they can be the same."

"I don't know, exactly."

"Okay, let's say it costs as much as your field hockey stick—and you can keep the hockey stick or get the guitar. Which do you choose?"

"Not fair!"

Well, no one said it was easy. In fact, Blake was correct: Any decision by her parents to force her to choose is, by definition, arbitrary; we don't have to give up the hockey stick to get the guitar, and she knows it. By the same token, any requirement that she "earn" the guitar by doing chores around the house is also arbitrary, since she isn't creating anything of value that can be swapped for the instrument.

Even so, the lesson is real. And so are the implications, which have been torturing economics students for decades. The opportunity-cost model, for example, confuses a lot of people because it seems to require that the quantity of valuable things stay fixed and unchanging, but while we know that wealth can and does increase *over time*, at any given *point in time*—which is where we buy and sell stuff—it actually is fixed. If it isn't scarce in the short term, it isn't really valuable.

Teaching Blake and Scott about the inescapable reality of scarcity and the importance of choice—that they can't have their cake and eat it too—is one of the most important jobs Penelope and I have. Whenever it becomes too much of a challenge, we console ourselves with the thought that they will figure it out. And with one other thought:

Since *everyone* has a different set of opportunity costs (Blake and Scott would rather have an ice cream than a dollar, but the ice cream shop would rather have the dollar), it stands to reason not just that choice matters but that choices made by individuals are light-years more efficient than those made by bureaucrats. Once Blake and Scott learn that, they'll be several laps ahead of virtually every elected official in the country.

Smith, Adam. Scottish philosopher (1723–90) and the founder of the discipline of economics. Author of *An Inquiry into the Nature and Causes of the Wealth of Nations*.

Even a decade before *The Wealth of Nations* (in which he wrote, "The property which every man has in his own labour, as it is the original foundation of all other property, so it is the most sacred and inviolable"), Smith was on record as arguing that the first priority of government "is to prevent the members of a society from incroaching on one another's property." But Smith's great insight was that the two conditions needed for the maximum amount of national wealth were perfect competition (or as close as possible to perfect) and complete freedom of buyers to substitute one commodity for another (or as close as possible to complete). This is how Smith's famous "invisible hand" forces **prices** and **profit** to their lowest possible level.

Though Smith didn't realize it, he was living in the first human era in which wealth, profit, and competition all started to grow over time. What he *did* realize is that the invisible hand is a much better tool for creating wealth than the visible hand—that without direction, control, or even goodwill, human self-interest is by far the most powerful force for human prosperity.

Stimulus, fiscal. Noun. An increase in government spending or decrease in taxes taken to limit the damage of an economic recession.

Of all the things that define economic Progressivism, maybe the most dangerous is its belief in the ability of government to do things more effectively than the marketplace. One example of this "we know what's best" arrogance is the enthusiasm with which Progressives support stimulating the economy by increasing spending—*always* with borrowed money—to minimize the damage of economic crises. While a case can be made for this (there are some places government spends money that can, theoretically, make a nation richer, as with roads and dams), it's not especially strong. Even if all the stimulus spending went toward improving infrastructure, the choices made about where to build bridges, harbors, and power-generating stations are always political and by definition less efficient, as with the $400 million bridge to Alaska's Gravina Island—one of the best-known "bridges to nowhere" but by no means the only one.

For reasons only they understand, Progressives always prefer spending a dollar as a stimulus rather than cutting a dollar in taxes, even though the two actions are mathematically identical. This is because they get hives at the idea that individuals know better than bureaucrats how to spend money.

Supply and demand. Noun. A way of comparing the two components by which markets determine prices.

The "law" of supply and demand is not exactly what a physicist would recognize as either a law or a theory. Actually, it's a picture: a graph.

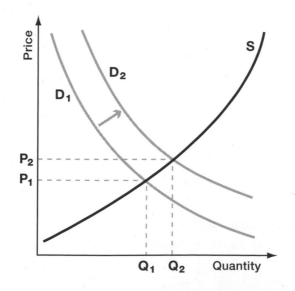

The vertical measurement here is price, the horizontal one quantity. The black curve represents supply, the gray demand. The point where they intersect is where the price and supply are in equilibrium. Clear, right?

Okay, try it this way. This supply curve says that, as the price of widgets goes up, widget manufacturers make more of them. As the price goes down, widget buyers buy more. The process stops when the two lines cross. However, if something happens to increase demand—widgets are discovered to clear up acne, eliminate belly fat, and remove those embarrassing wrinkles—the price *and* the supply will increase. If, on the other hand, something happens to increase the supply of widgets (a new manufacturing process or discovery of a new source of widget raw material), the price will fall.

Governments that ignore this basic relationship do so at their peril but don't always understand why. Progressives in general, and the current administration in particular, are always eager to find a commodity for which supply and demand are out of balance and blame that imbalance on too little regulation. The most upside-down version of this is probably health care, for which there is essentially infinite demand but also finite supply and a price that isn't paid by the consumer; anywhere buyers can't communicate their demand (by the price they're willing to pay) the result is chaos.

"Dad?"

"Yes, Blake?"

"You know all those words we've been writing down?"

"Sure I do."

"Well, I get it that some of them are things everyone agrees about, like 'interest' and 'price' . . . but lots of people disagree about the other stuff, right?"

"Yes, Blake. They do."

"So it's not like a dictionary that tells everyone the right meaning?"

That was a tough one. Do you admit to your daughter that lots of her parents' ideas are different from—for example—her teachers? Did I want her thinking it was all just a matter of opinion?

"Think of it this way, Blake. When people talk about profit, or regulation, the things they say depend on what they think is most important. If you think that the most important thing is keeping anybody from getting more than anyone else, then you think one thing. If you think the most important thing is letting everybody be as free as possible, you think another."

"And we believe in freedom, right?"

"Yup. We do."

CHAPTER 3

May 2009: The Properties of Property

As February 2009 turned into March, our township forester (yes, we have a township forester; don't you?) decided that a tree on our front lawn was diseased—and more important, that despite the fact that it looked to be on our property, it was in fact on the wrong side of the property line. Watching the tree being cut down gave Blake a pretty painful lesson in the difference between private and public property, but it did give us a chance to think about how important it was.

When economic writers use the term "building blocks" (for example, "property rights are one of the building blocks of free markets"), they're being metaphorical. In the Kernen household, we're more literal, as in "put those building blocks away . . . now!" It's not as if Blake doesn't have a strong sense of property rights. Or at least property. Our basement is so full of stuffed animals, plastic toys, fish tanks, and discarded electronics that you cannot see from one end to the other. And the sole reason that it isn't even more packed is that Blake has been filling it "only" for the last seven years. There's no problem explaining to her that things with value can be property.

On the other hand, they can also be not-property. Lots of things with value aren't property of any kind: You can't, for example, buy a child's hug, no matter how many commercials for Disney World suggest that you can. There's a long list of things that you can—sort of—buy, like better health, without being able to own them. You can buy a plane ticket to Hawaii, but that doesn't make a Hawaiian sunset into property.

So while we know that the fact that something has value, even monetary value, doesn't necessarily turn that something into property, we also know that a dining room table (or more to Blake's liking, an electric guitar) is property. There's something intuitive about at least some of the core ideas of property, something so basic that a fifth grader knows them without being told. If you possess something and no one else can use it without your permission—if you can, to put it in fifth-grader terms, tell your little brother to keep away from it—and you can buy it, sell it, or give it away, it's your property.

But an understanding of *property* isn't the same as understanding property *rights*, and explaining property rights to a ten-year-old turns out to be, well, challenging.

The Socratic method, for example, has its limits:

"Blake?"
"Yes, Dad?"
"Is that your game cartridge?"
"Uh-huh."
"What makes it yours?"
"Do you want me to put it away?"
"No. I want you to tell me why you think it's yours."
"You bought it for me."
"Whose was it before that?"
"GameStop's."
"And before that?"
"I'll put it away if you want."

....

The idea that a thing can be first the property of one person, then the property of another, seems like a good place to start. But do you have the same *right* to that property no matter how you came to possess it?

"Blake?"

"Yes, Dad?"

"If you had found the game cartridge lying on the street, would it still be yours?"

"I guess so."

"But not as much as if Mommy or I gave it to you?"

"Well, if someone was throwing it away, it'd be okay to take it. But if it was just lost, then maybe not."

"How about if you bought it with money you earned selling lemonade?"

"Then it would be mine, for sure."

"What would you call someone who took it away from you?"

"A thief, of course."

Out of the mouths of you-know-what.

For most of history, ownership was a might-makes-right concept. If you had something of value, and I took it because I was stronger than you, it was mine—at least unless someone even stronger made me give it back. The "someone" could be a tribal leader or a feudal lord or a modern state, but ownership was just possession with the permission of the biggest bully in the neighborhood.

Some people say—loudly—that nothing has really changed: that the government (usually, though not always, the federal government) is just the latest version of the biggest bully in the neighborhood. The press has taken to calling these people "conservative," but they're really not. There is a huge difference between a legitimate government restrained by the rule of law and a king restrained by nothing at all, and real conservatives understand that difference. The thing that separates liberals from free-market conservatives is not *whether* there should be some government-enforced rules about private property but *which* ones.

This turns out to be not so simple to figure out, much less explain to a ten-year-old. Possession, for example, which seems to be the simplest of all aspects of property, gets pretty blurry the closer you get to it: If our house is sitting on a piece of land for which we have a lease running ninety-nine years (which is more common than you'd think), who is the owner? Even if the owner of the land today is old Mr. Smithers, he is certainly not going to be in possession during his lifetime, nor will young Mr. Smithers.

So is the key element the ability to *use* the property? "Usufruct," a fine crossword-puzzle word meaning the use and enjoyment of the property of someone else, is a historically important right, but is a long way short of what we mean by "*property* rights." Closer is the right to transfer ownership: If you can legally sell something, it's awfully hard to argue that it isn't property; but there are so many ways we restrict the right to sell some forms of property—you can sell your blood but not your kidney—that it isn't especially helpful as a complete definition.

So I decided to try to let Blake figure out what sorts of things *should* be property and which shouldn't.

"Blake?"
"Yes, Dad?"
"Let's make a list."

I asked Blake to divide a piece of paper into two columns, with "things that we should be able to own" on the left, and "things we shouldn't be able to own" on the right. Here's what we came up with:

THINGS WE SHOULD OWN	THINGS NO ONE SHOULD OWN
Clothes	Air
Furniture	People
TV sets	Wild animals
Pets	Trees
Refrigerators	
Food	
Plates	
Computers	
House	
Backyard	

Blake's list was a pretty good summary of what our instincts tell us about property, but using it to derive some rules about what property means in a free-market economy wasn't all that easy.

So I did what I always do when I can't think of anything else to do.

"Blake?"

"Yes, Dad?"

"Let's take a walk."

It's only about a mile from our front door to the Short Hills Historical District—twenty minutes under normal circumstances, but twice as long when you do it accompanied by a four-foot-ten-inch girl who is fascinated by every flowering plant along the route. Or any kid, since one of the defining characteristics of childhood is a complete inability to stay on sidewalks or paths and off the neighbors' lawns. For a change, this habit was useful, because every time Blake strayed onto someone's property I was able to ask, "Is this your property?"

"No."

"Whose is it?"

"Whoever lives here."

"And before they lived here?"

"Whoever lived here then."

"And before anyone lived here?"

Unroll pretty much every idea we have about property—private *or* public—and you eventually come to land: "real" property. This isn't because it was the first kind of property. But all other forms of tangible property are obviously distinct from one another, so much so that no one argued about the *boundaries* of ownership; our ancestors might have fought about the ownership of a flint ax, but not about who owned the edge, for example. Land was different. Most pieces of desirable land tended to be right next to another piece, which demanded a more rigorous approach to defining precisely what the property *was*, and to this day the laws about buying and selling real estate are very different from those about buying and selling anything else.

You can buy a diamond ring or a car or even stock in a company with about one-tenth the amount of paper generated for even the smallest purchase of real estate. Someone has to certify that no one has any claims against the property. Someone else has to do the same for any of the property's previous owners. Most important, the extent of the property covered has to be very precisely surveyed. A house address isn't nearly enough; the deed of sale for a piece of real estate needs to be described using terminology that (in New Jersey, anyway) dates back to the Middle Ages. The county clerk's map tends to describe any particular lot with something like "beginning with the end of a stone wall on the south side of Washington Avenue, and following along the banks of Stony Creek for one mile northwest. . . ."*

---

* This is true in the Northeast, which I now know adopted the old English system, called "metes and bounds," in colonial times. Beginning in 1785, on territory that would become my home state of Ohio, the rest of the country was surveyed with a far more modern system: the Pubic Land Survey System.

Precise definitions of land boundaries were intended to resolve the earliest disputes about the line between "our" property and "yours." Creating them also forced people to think about the moment when land didn't belong to anyone, when it was (to people who can't resist using Latin, like lawyers) *res nullius*: a thing without an owner. One of the attractions of the New World to the Old was what looked like a couple of billion acres of *res nullius* land, and the first few centuries of European colonization were one big land grab, evicting the locals and claiming property as fast as the colonists could sharpen their quills.

That's the way it's taught in Blake's school, anyway. Probably your child's school, as well. This isn't exactly false, but it isn't completely true, either. All of the property along our walk—for miles in every direction—was transferred on July 11, 1666, when the Lenape Indians sold it to a syndicate of English colonists for a barrel of gunpowder, one hundred "barrs" of lead, twenty axes, twenty pistols, ten kettles, four barrels of beer, fifty knives, and a closetful of coats, breeches, and blankets.*

This is interesting not as a debate about whether the price was fair—Blake doesn't think so—or even whether the Lenapes had any clear title to the land in the first place. The misunderstanding about the settlement of North America goes deeper than that: a profound mistrust of the whole idea of private property, in which the Native American attitude toward land seems to reside on higher moral ground than that occupied by the rapacious European colonizers. Some of this is collateral damage from the environmental movement; some is just another bit of nostalgia for the *res nullius* of the Garden of Eden, a belief that the earth is treated better when no one owns any of it.

---

* The deed description, which I found in our local library, begins, "Bounded and limited with the bay eastward and the great River Pesayak northward, to the great Creke or River in the meadow, running to the head of the Cove, and from thence bareing a westerly line for the south bound, which said great Creek is commonly called. . . ."

We actually know what happens to land when it isn't anyone's property, and it's not exactly the Garden of Eden. Consider Blake's trees, for example. Deforestation wasn't invented by capitalism, but it *was* a widespread human activity for thousands of years; virtually all of the trees of central and western Europe were cut down (for fuel, for building, and for charcoal) between the eighth and fifteenth centuries. And they weren't replaced, since the logging was performed by people with no stake in the future of those forests.

Don't like trees? You can't go into a fancy restaurant these days without being lectured on the "sustainability" of this or that fish species, but the reason that fisheries are so difficult to sustain is that it's so hard for anyone to treat fish like property, which makes their survival hostage to something other than self-interest. And it's always going to make sense to some fishermen to take everything possible out of the ocean, even to the point of collapse, since the costs of that collapse are shared by everyone who makes a living from the sea but the benefits go to the most aggressive. This was what the environmentalist Garrett Hardin called the "tragedy of the commons" in an essay he wrote in 1968: the idea that where everyone grazes cattle on common land, it's in the interest of any one of them to eat the grass down to the dirt before anyone else does so.

You probably guessed his solution (if you didn't, go back and re-read the word "environmentalist"): the maximum amount of government intervention. People must be told how much they are allowed to take from the earth, since otherwise they will turn it into a sterile desert.* Like, for example, Oregon, where a property right in timber is so well recognized that there are more trees *planted* there every year than clear-cutting took out of all of New England in a century.

---

* Hardin was nothing if not consistent, contending in the same article that the same logic argued for government control of reproduction, with the famous argument that there is "no right to breed." The Nobel Prize–winning economist Elinor Ostrom demonstrated why, despite Hardin's logic, the world was not, in fact, a desert . . . but he is still regarded as a hero of the environmental movement.

And it isn't just trees. North America's bison population, which numbered as many as thirty million in 1700, was reduced to as few as one thousand by the 1890s. Our local supermarket sells, at $5.98 a pound, ground bison meat,* and not because of the 35,000 or so that have been restored to Yellowstone and other national parks but because of the *500,000* now raised for consumption—a powerful reminder that rational self-interest is a more durable protector of the environment than sentiment.

That's true whether we're talking about Oregon timber or Wyoming bison or New Jersey residences: Once something is property, it tends to find its way to the person who puts the highest value on it. That's what happened to Hobart Road, where Blake and I were walking (a route that I had taken the precaution of researching beforehand; sometimes I am not so dumb).

Virtually all of Short Hills is built on property acquired in the 1870s by a businessman named Stewart Hartshorn, whose venture into the development business was fueled by a recognition that this particular piece of land might find its most highly valued function as what he called "a harmonious community for people who appreciate nature." The center of that community was our destination, and it says a lot about the way in which one sort of valuable property—land—can be transformed into something even more valuable, enriching not only the person who performs the transformation but his customers as well.

The characteristic of the acreage that was most appealing to Hartshorn, as he later recalled, was its beauty: the rolling green hills that would give the community its name (local residents remain grateful that he resisted the temptation to name it "Hartshornville"). But there are dozens of equally pretty spots throughout northern New Jersey. The *real* appeal of this particular bit of property was its proximity to the Morris & Essex Railroad, which had been running

---

* For more about the Kernen family's eating habits, see chapter 8.

between Newark and Morristown since 1836, less than a decade after the world's first regularly scheduled steam railway started running between Manchester and Liverpool. That's why the center of the Short Hills Historical District is the place where Hartshorn built a station on the line, to carry the residents of his hoped-for community to Newark and, via ferry, to New York. Nor did he stop there; by the time he finished his first seventeen houses, he had opened a sawmill to cut lumber and a quarry to mine limestone for the community's houses, then selling for between three and four thousand dollars. (Hartshorn was not so dumb, either.) The conversion of one sort of valuable property—trees and stone—into a far more valuable sort—houses—is the magic of free markets, but it is utterly dependent upon respect for private property and the ability to buy it and sell it.

Some people value the natural world only when it is left untouched by humans. The impulse has its positive side, as anyone who has ever visited a national park can testify. But unless you are the sort of environmentalist who thinks the planet would be better off with no humans at all (and if so, you're probably not reading this anyway), you're aware that humans are part of the natural world. And that the natural world can be a pretty hard place. Animals and plants have been eating one another ever since there have been animals and plants, following a pattern first exhibited by bacteria and other one-celled organisms. The idea that nature exists in some sort of harmonious balance is nothing more than sentimentality, which is why life forms were going extinct for billions of years before the first humans appeared.

To be fair, the only thing that distinguished those first humans from locusts was that they were far more successful, spreading to every corner of the globe in what is the geologic equivalent of an eyeblink. They didn't just destroy an entire continent's worth of trees; they decimated populations of animals both by hunting them to extinction and by occupying their habitats.

On the other hand, there *is* another thing that separates humans—modern humans—from the rest of the natural world. Once humans recognize property rights in land, they start to protect that land. And once they get rich enough to do so, they preserve it, as well. This isn't just Kernen family gossip: The Heritage Foundation and the *Wall Street Journal* have been issuing a report for the last fifteen years that pretty conclusively shows that the richer a nation gets, the stronger its environmental protections. The Environmental Performance Index, which is published annually by the World Economic Forum, the Center for International Earth Science Information Network (CIESIN), and the Yale Center for Environmental Law and Policy shows essentially the same thing.

So did Stewart Hartshorn. His community was explicitly planned not just to preserve the existing natural beauties of the area but to cultivate them. Hanging in our local historical society is a picture, dated 1878, of the road along which Blake and I were walking.

"Dad?"

"Yes, Blake?"

"What happened to all the trees?"

Fewer than half the trees that shaded us on our walk were visible. Their predecessors—owned by no one—had been cut down for firewood long ago. Only when Stewart Hartshorn's community was established did the owners of the property recognize the ornamental value of trees. Which is when they started nurturing them—another object lesson in the social value of property rights.

(An even better one is the seventeen acres that Hartshorn's daughter, Cora, bequeathed to Short Hills as an "Arboretum, Wildflower and bird sanctuary," which is not only precisely the sort of public asset that is the direct consequence of putting private property to work but also Blake's favorite place in all of Short Hills.)

....

"Dad?"

"Yes, Blake?"

"How did Mr. Hartshorn get the money to buy the land in the first place?"

As it turns out, the source of Hartshorn's original stake offers an even more interesting insight into the nature of property than his career as a developer, though in this case, the property was pretty abstract. Hartshorn, you see, was an inventor.

Given the thousands of years in which people have been describing, disputing, and discovering value in property, it's something of a surprise to realize that we've recognized that ideas are a valuable sort of property themselves—maybe the most valuable of all—for only a few centuries. England's first patent law was drafted in 1628, but two hundred years later, when the first steam engines were driving the first locomotives across the English countryside, only about four thousand patents had been granted. That was enough, however, to ignite the Industrial Revolution, which would take the worldwide average GDP when Stewart Hartshorn was born in 1845—about $1,000 a year, still a considerable increase from the $700 to $800 at which it had been frozen for centuries—and more than double it by the time he died in 1935.[*]

Hartshorn's invention wasn't exactly the steam engine. When he was not yet twenty, he invented a mechanical window shade—or in the type of language beloved of patent lawyers, "the application of a pawl and ratchet or notched hub, arranged in such a manner that the shade may be stopped and retained at any desired height or point within the scope of its movement by a single manipulation of the shade, the usual cord for operating or turning the shade-roller being

---

[*] Since then, it has, in constant dollars, more than quintupled. Thank you, inventors.

dispensed with entirely, as well as counterpoises, which had in some instances been employed, in connection with spring rollers, for holding the shade at the desired point."

The Hartshorn roller shade was successful enough that its design long survived the patent protection it was given in 1864; it was essentially the same design still in use when I was young enough to be scared out of my wits every time the roller pulled the window shade up with a sound like a gunshot. Hartshorn's creation made him far wealthier than his career as a real estate developer. His experience was a small, though profitable, example of the "discovery" of a right to intellectual property, one that was unknown to Galileo or Leonardo or a thousand generations of anonymous innovators. All of them, you see, lived in a time when the only way to make a living as an inventor was to either find a rich patron or keep your invention secret, neither of which was an especially good incentive to treat inventions as property able to be bought and sold.

Once inventions began to be treated as property, the same thing happened to them that happened to every other sort of property: When people can buy and sell ideas, they start producing more of them. A lot more. Hartshorn's roller-shade patent was the 44,624th issued by the U.S. Patent and Trademark Office in the seventy-three years from its inception in 1789, almost immediately after the Constitution (which granted the national government a right to issue patents and copyrights) was ratified.

This is one of the most counterintuitive things about property specifically and free markets generally. Every other competing economic system assumes that things of value are finite: that when you consume something, you leave behind less than when you started. But as mankind has found more and more ways to recognize property rights in goods, the opposite has happened. Once someone can own them, we get more trees, more crops—and more (and more valuable) ideas.

Easy to see, when you think about it. Hard to explain, however, to a ten-year-old.

. . . .

"Blake, you know we use oil and coal and natural gas for energy, right?"

"Electric cars don't."

"Even electric cars need to get energy from power plants, and they burn coal and oil and gas."

"Okay."

"Do you know where we get the fuel from?"

"The ground?"

"Pretty much. Most of it has been in the ground for hundreds of millions of years, and it takes million of years to produce more."

"I *know* that."

"So . . . when someone drills a hole in the surface of the earth and takes oil or coal out of it, is there more or less left behind?"

"Less, of course."

"So what would you say if I told you that we've been drilling for oil for a hundred years, and there's a lot *more* oil now than there was a hundred years ago?"

Blake said nothing, though her expression told me she knew she was being tricked but didn't know how. She has a lot of company. Most people don't understand how proven oil reserves have grown over time, even as humanity has burned more and more oil. We have been compelled for decades to listen to constant alarms about impending shortages of oil (and gas and cadmium and rare earth and lithium . . .). It's only common sense, after all: The planet isn't producing any more oil, or anything else, so it stands to reason that if we started with x tons of palladium, for example, in the earth's crust, and we use five thousand ounces a year (mostly for the catalytic converters in cars), there must be five thousand fewer ounces left behind. After a while, we'll run out.

Only we don't. Back in 1980, the economist Julian Simon made a famous bet with the biologist and scarcitymonger Paul Ehrlich:

He allowed Ehrlich, who had predicted worldwide famines and resource shortages for years, to pick any basket of commodities and hold them for ten years. If the prices increased because of those Ehrlich-promised shortages, he would pay the difference; if they decreased, Ehrlich would do the same. When the price of every one of Ehrlich's picks—copper, tungsten, chromium, nickel, and tin—fell (tin, which traded for nearly $9 per pound in 1980, was only $3.88 in 1990)—he lost, though he's still predicting imminent worldwide resource shortages, despite a record of doomsaying that is so far untarnished by success.

The reason why Ehrlich lost—why "shortages" are always (at worst) temporary—is central to understanding free markets: So long as people have incentives to find a commodity, in the form of a price that is greater than the cost of finding it, they'll do so. In economic terms, there are no shortages; there is simply a lag while price catches up to demand, and once it does, inventive people go get it.

So long as they are permitted to assert a property right over what they find. Sometimes they can't. Sometimes it's impractical to divvy up something of value so that people can assert a property right to it, either because the value of the commodity is less than the cost of policing it—that's why European and the northeastern U.S. forests were clear-cut*—or because technology hasn't caught up with the potential for "propertizing" something.

Which is what happened to television.

When I tell Blake about growing up with only seven television channels to choose from, she gets the same look she had when I tried to prove to her that the earth seems to have, in economic terms, more oil now than when John D. Rockefeller started up Standard Oil of

---

* It's also, in a very different setting, why you can buy a reserved seat for a play but not for a movie: It costs just as much to hire ushers to make sure that no one sits in your $10 seat at the local multiplex as it does to hire ushers to make sure no one sits in your $100 seat in a Broadway theater.

New Jersey. The remote control that operates the Kernen multimedia center not only has two dozen buttons operating previously unknown functions with mysterious acronyms like "CC," "DVR," "REC," and "PIP" but also is capable of accessing more than fifteen hundred channels (and will probably, by the time you read this, have even more.)

The introduction of a technology that could slice the electromagnetic spectrum into fine enough bands that a thousand different programs could be produced and sent into people's homes hasn't always been greeted with applause, particularly by America's elites. However, it's a stretch to argue that the quality of programming back in the "vast wasteland" days of the 1960s was better; I mean, I loved *The Beverly Hillbillies*, but then I was also ten years old. Does anyone really believe that *Playhouse 90* was better than *The Wire*? More instructively, the way in which the government involved itself in broadcasting when the airwaves were—sort of—regarded as a public asset was profoundly different. Back then, the only way to make sure that the electromagnetic frequency used to send *The Beverly Hillbillies* into your home did so without interference from another frequency was by the most heavy-handed government regulation. In return for a giveaway of a hugely valuable band on the spectrum—a giveaway that was, as such giveaways always are, determined by political clout rather than economic efficiency—the networks were obliged, for example, to submit to censorship of a sort that the modern cable system laughs at.

The lesson seems obvious, and not just to those of us who cash paychecks produced by cable-TV revenue: The more programming channels are treated as private property, rather than the gift of the government, the better: for diversity, for quality, and certainly for quantity. Ted Koppel may complain—okay, he *does* complain—that TV news has deteriorated to the point that people no longer watch to get the facts but to reinforce their prejudices, but our local cable provider now offers more than five times as many hours of news every day than it did when *Nightline* went on the air—and if some of that news has a strong point of view, at least someone admits it, which sounds to me a lot better than *pretending* to be objective.*

You can't really debate whether private property has increased human welfare everywhere it has been recognized; it's obvious to anyone with eyes to see. There is, however, another debate, which is whether property rights are justified *only* because of their impact on prosperity.

That would seem to be enough, and maybe it is. But for the last three centuries, some really smart people have been arguing about whether property is good for reasons having nothing to do with more GDP. The English physician and philosopher John Locke, for example, thought that property rights were natural, not just efficient. His thinking went something like this:

1. God created the world.
2. Anything created by God was, by definition, not legitimately owned by anyone.
3. But we want and need ownership.
4. So property exists whenever the work of man is mixed with the work of God.

This was, by any measure, revolutionary: Labor, not just prior possession, was what made ownership legitimate. Land was common property, but the *improvements* in land that made it valuable—from plowed fields to fortified castles—were private property, the natural right of whoever improved it. Discoveries of natural phenomena were *res nullius*; but anything that made them useful was property.

---

* Old-school guys like Koppel probably even believe in their own objectivity, which is the saddest part of all. For more about media confusion, see chapter 5.

Locke's argument wasn't accepted by everyone, even people who accepted the importance of work in justifying ownership. Contemporaries of Locke (such as David Hume) and later thinkers (such as Karl Marx) agreed that labor added value but not that it granted a natural right to property. Even so, Locke's theory seems to be the one that makes the most sense of Blake's list: Clothes are property because they are made (and subsequently sold). People are not because they are the work of God.

But wild animals?

"Do you mean *all* wild animals, Blake? Birds?"

"Of course."

"What about fish?"

"Yup."

"What about the one you caught?"

"I threw him back."

"But you could have eaten him if you wanted."

"Ewww."

One day, Blake pulled a smallmouth bass out of our local pond that was definitely big enough to make for good eating . . . if, in fact, she liked to eat fish, which she does not. This saved me from having to teach her how to clean and gut a fish, at least for now, but seemed to be a teachable moment nonetheless.

"So it's okay to hunt, Blake?"

"Well . . . I wouldn't like to, but I guess. If it was someone's work."

"And if that someone shoots a deer?"

"They'd get to keep it."

"So it wasn't property when it was alive, but it turned into property after it was dead?"

"Uh-huh."

"Why?"

"Well, it was their work. Just like planting flowers. Or raising cattle."

One of the virtues of educating a child in the labor theory of value (or letting her do it herself) is that it is a constant reminder of the value of hard work; Blake knows that anything done half assed—one of her favorite phrases, even if it embarrasses her to repeat it—is only half valuable. But it also teaches that the legitimate owner of anything valuable—of any property—is the individual who created that value by adding his or her work to the work of nature. There's nothing wrong with governments protecting the "rights" of the natural world, but they have no natural right to the value created by work, and when they assert one—when politicians debate how much of the national wealth to return to its creators—they are, as Blake reminded me, nothing but bullies.

"Dad?"

"Yes, Blake?"

"If work is what makes something property, then is work a *kind* of property?"

"Yeah. I think so."

"So my homework is my property?"

"Well . . . yes. So long as you accept that your mother and I have the right to inspect it."

"So if it's called homework, how come I don't get paid?"

CHAPTER 4

October 2009: Who Made My Shoelaces?

October 2009: Our son, Scott, learns to tie his shoes, and a whole lot more . . .

Among all the purchases made by the Kernen family over the course of a year, this one had to be one of the most mundane: a pair of shoelaces for Blake's brother, Scott. Actually, two pairs. Three bucks at any drugstore, supermarket, or even shoe store in America. Or, in fact, around the entire world. Billions of them are made and sold every year, from the most primitive outdoor market to the newest upscale mall, and by innumerable Internet retailers.

They've been around quite a while, as well. A couple of years ago, archaeologists found a leather shoe in present-day Armenia that was made more than five thousand years ago, and not only does it look no more beat up than Scott's sneakers after a day playing in the mud, but it was held together with, you guessed it, laces. Shoes using eyelets and cross-lacing have been around since at least the twelfth century. Shoelaces are what you might call a mature technology.

And no one knows how to make them. Or more accurately, "not a single person on the face of the earth knows how to make" them.

That "not a single person" line is taken from an essay written by a man named Leonard Read in 1958. Titled "I, Pencil: My Family Tree as Told to Leonard E. Read," it is a short but illuminating explanation of the miraculous way in which technology, raw materials, transportation, and science are brought together by literally millions of people to manufacture a simple "lead" (really graphite) pencil, and how, even though every one of those millions knows a little bit about the processes involved, no one knows the whole story. More to the point—this is an essay about free markets, after all, one regularly cited by Milton Friedman—it is about how those millions of people, and their transactions, somehow manage to organize themselves to produce that pencil, without, as Read puts it, any "master mind . . . dictating or forcibly directing" them.

And I thought that there wasn't any better way to show Blake and Scott the incredible power of an undirected free market than with a pair of shoelaces.

The particular shoelaces used for the exercise weren't anything special: two thirty-six-inch lengths of cotton and polyester, capped with acetate tips and packaged on a couple of inches of cardboard. But their journey to Scott's shoes took us on a trip around the world and through a whole lot of centuries.

Cotton first:

"Scott?"

"Yeah?"

"Do you know what this is?"

"Uh, a string?"

"If it were still in a sneaker, you'd know, wouldn't you?"

"It's a shoelace!"

"You bet it is. And it's partly made out of cotton. You know what cotton is?

"Like cotton balls?"

"Just like."

....

Actually, cotton balls are the product that most closely resembles the most valuable part of the plant before it gets processed. As with any other form of life, all parts of the cotton plant are pretty useful, but the one that matters to the shoelace manufacturer (in fact, to anyone who wants to turn cotton into money) is the seedpod, which is roughly the size and shape of the cotton balls we keep in the bathroom and is responsible for contributing several hundred billion dollars to the world's economy every year. The pods—the bolls—are where the plant grows something that looks like hair: fibers a couple of inches long. Since those hairs have to be spun into yarn, the plants that had the longest ones—"long-staple" cotton—were the most popular ones for thousands of years until a onetime tutor from Massachusetts named Eli Whitney invented his first cotton gin in 1794.

Whitney's invention—hooks attached to a rotating cylinder next to a wire screen—wasn't something anyone told him to create. His moment of revelation—he watched a cat try to pull a bird through a wire fence, leaving a bunch of feathers behind—came because he realized that the short-staple cotton of Georgia and South Carolina would be worth a *lot* more money if someone could separate it from its seeds.

And it was. The gins of Gujarat, India, where the cotton in Scott's shoelaces comes from, are more than just bigger, higher-powered versions of Whitney's original; modern cotton-stripping machines pound the cotton with rollers, bats, and brushes and knock the cleaned bolls onto a conveyer, but the principle is the same. The shoelace manufacturers don't need to know much about growing cotton, though, any more than the cotton farmers need to know how to make a shoelace.

They *do* have to know how to raise a crop of cotton bolls before bollworms—moth larvae, an even bigger threat today than the boll weevil that terrified cotton farmers in the early part of the twentieth century—can eat the profits right out from under them. Spraying cotton plants with insecticides, though, has a lot of nasty side effects, which is why some really clever chemists came up with a new variety of cotton that modified the plant's DNA so it could produce a bacterium with the tongue-twisting name *B. thuringiensis*. No central planner told the folks at Monsanto to come up with Bt cotton,* and neither the cotton farmer not the shoelace maker really knows—or needs to know—how they did it.

Cleaning cotton is only the first step on the way to Scott's shoes, though. Those two- to three-inch-long fibers need to be twisted, or spun, at an angle into a much longer and stronger thread, or yarn. The yarn then needs to be woven—with polyester filaments, about which more below—into the quarter-inch-wide strings that can eventually hold a shoe on an eight-year-old foot.

Indian cotton workers have been using spinning wheels and spindles to spin high-quality cotton for centuries—so much so that Great Britain passed laws in 1700 and 1720 to prohibit imports of the stuff from its own colony. But India's productivity advantage (essentially a really huge labor force; a lot of India's productivity still depends on its population) had vanished by the late eighteenth century, when a bunch of British inventors came up with a whole raft of inventions to automate the spinning and weaving process: the spinning jenny, for example, a spinning wheel turned on its side, operating multiple spindles simultaneously, and powered by either water or steam. Or the "mule," which tied a spindle carriage to a loom, or weaving frame, and was therefore able to convert cotton into cloth in one powered operation.

India's cotton producers got the message, though not as a result of central planning. The country is now covered with cotton mills that use the latest version of this technology to produce thirty-five

---

* Central planners *have* been attacking Bt cotton pretty regularly, though, despite its demonstrated ability to improve yields using far less toxic insecticides. Central planners tend to be Progressives, and Progressives haven't got a lot of love for genetically modified organisms, or GMOs.

million bales—a bale of cotton is about five hundred pounds—annually, for everything from sailcloth to underwear . . . to shoelaces.

Of course, the woven fibers that will eventually become Scott's shoelaces wouldn't really pass muster unless we could buy them in a color he found appealing: bright red. The manufacture of dyes that are used to turn the dirty-white color of the natural cotton into something that could be used on a fire engine is a pretty huge industry itself. The Gujarat plants that supply the dye—"direct dye," which bonds chemically to the cotton fibers—to the neighboring cotton mills are, like the farmers planting genetically modified seeds, the inheritors of thousands of years of applied science. Also, they don't care about shoelaces, but they *love* vivid colors. Come to think of it, just like Scott.

But neither the cotton farmer nor the mill worker (nor the manufacturers of the picking, spinning, or weaving equipment, much less the inventors of the original technology behind Bt cotton or the automated looms) actually has any interest in shoelaces. Each of them performs a single indispensable function and neither knows or needs to know anything much about the stuff everyone else is doing.

"So, Scott, now that you know how cotton balls get turned into the kind of fabric that we're going to make your shoelaces from, I've got another question for you."

"Okay."

"How many people, do you think, does it take to just grow, spin, and weave the cotton?"

"Five thousand? No . . . five million? No . . . a *billion*!"

"Let's just use the small number for now. What that means is that five thousand people get up every morning and go plant or pick or spin cotton, some of which is going to end up in your shoelaces. My question is: How do they know what to do?"

While some shoelaces are made out of 100 percent cotton, Scott's are made out a combination of cotton and polyester, which is one of a whole lot of products we call "synthetic" but whose raw material was originally organic: crude oil.

Here's how it works: The oil that's pumped out of the ground—in Saudi Arabia, for example—is like a really complicated stew, the ingredients of which are valuable for something used in making a pair of shoelaces. The "lightest" parts (the ones that are lightest in color are the ones with the most carbon) are the easiest to burn, so they're turned into the gasoline that powers the trucks that carry the components of those simple laces (also the aviation fuel used on airfreight carriers and the diesel used by ships and trains). The darker parts, though, are just as important. Making the molecules that will turn into the polyester that is combined with the cotton in Scott's laces is the job of both the refineries that "unmix" the stew (the process is called "fractional distillation") and the petrochemical plants that take the heavier parts of the crude oil and turn them into propene, and eventually polyester.

"So, Scott, where do your shoelaces come from?"
"Arabia?"

Not yet, they don't. The petrochemical plant where the polypropylene is manufactured is in China, in a place called Jinjiang City. The thousands of people who work in the plant *wear* shoes, of course, but they don't have to know that part of their job is making the stuff that will be attached to the shoelaces that keep the shoes on their feet. They just have to know that there's a buyer for their plastics and a seller where they can, in turn, buy their raw materials.

"How *do* they know what to do?"
"Do you think someone is telling everyone what to do, Scott?"
"Yeah! That's it."
"Who?"
"The president? No . . . the richest man in the world?"

"Neither one. In fact, no one is telling them what to do, or rather, everyone is telling everyone what to do."

"I don't get it."

Those shoelaces weren't, of course, just hanging on a shelf all by themselves. They were attached to a piece of cardboard that told us how long they were, how much they cost, and who made them (and, luckily for me, *where* they were made).

The cardboard didn't come from Arabia or China or India, though. *That* piece of the story took us to a pulp mill in Canada, where trees are turned into paper. Those shoelaces, therefore, are indirectly depending on hundreds of *other* machines: In pulp mills, debarkers remove the bark from trees, chippers turn the remaining wood into usable sizes, and digesters use chemicals to transform the chips into something resembling wet oatmeal. And then, in the paper mill, a single machine uses rollers, dryers, and formers to convert the wet oatmeal okay, the slurry—into all kinds of paper—in the case of Scott's shoelaces, cardboard.

By now, the yarn, plastic, and cardboard have traveled just about halfway around the world, encountering thousands (at least) of people operating different machines at just about every stop. I suppose someone could make a shoelace or a shoe—or even Leonard Read's pencil—by hand. No one does. There are literally thousands of different machines needed, from the cotton harvesters (which not only pick the cotton bolls but also remove their seeds) to the automated spinning and weaving machines that turn it into yarn and cloth. Then there are the oil derricks and pumps that extract oil from under the sand and the fractional distillers that turn crude oil into dozens of different products: fuel to operate the trucks, ships, and trains that transport every item needed for Scott's shoelaces, and also the detergents that clean them and the plastic used for the polyester in the fabric. Other machinery is used to turn trees into cardboard and cotton/polyester into yarn.

None of the people who manufacture (or even operate) those machines know much about anything but their own little piece of the operation, of course. They don't even know anything about the equipment by which the steel used to make them is made from the iron dug out of mines all over the world and melted into something called "pig" iron: the open hearths, blast and arc furnaces, and rolling mills. Scott's shoelaces even need machines to make *other* machines: lathes, shapers, grinders, and dozens more (most of them now operated by computers, but you get the idea).

Up to this point, however, Scott's five thousand (or one billion) workers have been sort of laboring in the dark. Only at the last stop—the shoelace factory—do people really see the final product. That's where shoelace-braiding machines, each of which looks like a really big wagon wheel laid on its side, weave those polyester-cotton yarns from India together like ribbons round a maypole. A long string—a *very* long string—emerges from each machine every twenty seconds or so.

Then a different machine puts acetate tips—which I've just learned are called aglets—on them.* It dips the braided strings in a solvent called acetone (yet another petrochemical made from polypropylene), heats the acetate, and wraps it around the braids at intervals that are the length of Scott's shoelaces. What comes out the other end is a long piece of shoelace with a transparent acetate band every few feet, and when the bands are cut in half, so are the braids. Presto: shoelaces.

One more machine later—the pairing machine—the shoelaces are wound into pairs, sent to the blister-packing machine, heat-sealed in plastic (more petrochemicals), put in boxes (more cardboard), and sent to a loading dock, where trucks pick them up.

---

* Acetate actually comes from the same wood-pulp mill as the raw material for the cardboard with which the laces are packaged.

....

"Got it now?"

"Nope."

"What don't you understand?"

"How can everyone tell everyone else what to do at the same time?"

I sometimes think that Scott's question underlines the biggest difference between Progressives and free-market conservatives. The idea is pretty counterintuitive, after all: How *can* such a system function at all, much less provide the abundance that permits, for example, a pair of shoelaces to be available wherever and whenever anyone needs them?

The key is information: Information is what allows a cotton farmer or oil refiner or lumber mill to decide how much they should be selling to the dozens of manufacturers who eventually use their raw materials to make a pair of shoelaces. Scott's notion—that the president or the "richest man in the world" can provide that information—is, essentially, the argument for socialism: Government bureaucrats can do the job best.

Now, I know that Progressives aren't all, or maybe even mostly, socialists, but that's a little like saying that they only have a chronic head cold instead of tuberculosis. When it comes to the economy, Progressives have a reflexive distrust of the market, and for the same reason that Scott does: They believe that it's just as sensible to trust an economic system designed and operated by no one as it is to be a passenger in a car without a driver. Progressives, who are reliably hostile to the idea of intelligent design in human evolution, are positively ecstatic about it in economic planning.

Of course, intelligent design in biology at least argues that the designer is divine and resides in heaven; in Progressive economics, it just assumes that the designer has a PhD and lives in Washington, DC.

The counterargument—that economies not only don't *need* a designer but do better *without* one—is that prices and information are, essentially, two ways of talking about the same thing. This is because cotton or oil or wood can only be compared in terms of the money someone is willing to pay for them. When farmers decide how much cotton to ship to the mill that will, eventually, turn it into the yarn in Scott's shoelaces (or, for that matter, how much cotton to plant, as opposed to some other crop), they get the information they need from the price that the cotton can command.

More than sixty years ago, the political philosopher Friedrich Hayek* showed that prices, therefore, were a kind of index to all the local and personal knowledge about what people want. He called this self-organizing system catallaxy: "the order brought about by the mutual adjustment of many individual economies in a market."

Well, he wasn't always a very good phrasemaker, but the idea is more important than the word.

"Think of this another way, Scott. When you want to buy a new video game—"

"Spider-Man?"

"Okay. Spider-Man. When you go to the store, and you want to buy one, but they don't have a copy for sale, what happens?"

"They get more copies?"

"Right. From where?"

"Activision!"

"And what does Activision do?"

"They make more?"

"They do indeed. Your wanting the game is how they know how many to make, but they only know if you offer to pay for it."

"Okay."

---

* For more about Hayek, see chapter 2.

"But now imagine that even more people want another game from Activision, like Call of Duty. Now they can only make so many copies, so they have to use all this information to decide whether to make more copies of Spider-Man or Call of Duty—and maybe they don't make enough copies of Spider-Man."

"Not fair!"

Sigh. Well, that's why the Progressive agenda still has so many supporters, despite a century's worth of experience with central planning (North Korea, anyone?). To anyone who wants what he wants when he wants it—and at the price he wants—the market can seem a little, well, unfair.

But *everything* seems unfair to someone. To me, a fair exchange is one where the thing I sell is worth more than the thing I buy—and vice versa. The more things everyone has to freely buy and sell, the fairer the system is.

A free market produces just about everything more efficiently than any other system, but it might be that the most important thing it produces is information: It turns out that millions (or billions) of people choosing where to spend their money creates a gigantic pool of information that millions (or billions) of people can use to choose where to invest their labor and resources. The way to produce the kind of abundance that makes $3 shoelaces and $50 video games available is actually pretty simple, though hard to understand: Just get out of the way and let the information flow both ways, in the form of price signals. That's how the self-organizing magic works.

This is what Adam Smith had in mind more than two centuries ago when he described the "invisible hand"—you know, the one that produces infinitely more than any visible one. Here's how Smith put it: Every individual is led by "an invisible hand to promote an end which was no part of his intention. Nor is it always the worse for the society that it was no part of it. By pursuing his own interest he frequently promotes that of the society more effectually than when he really intends to promote it. . . . It is not from the benevolence of the butcher, the brewer, or the baker, that we expect our dinner, but from their regard to their own interest"

Or as Leonard Read ended *I, Pencil*:

> The lesson I have to teach is this: *Leave all creative energies uninhibited.* Merely organize society to act in harmony with this lesson. Let society's legal apparatus remove all obstacles the best it can. Permit these creative know-hows freely to flow. Have faith that free men and women will respond to the Invisible Hand.

You bet. No matter how much evidence you muster to show that leaving "all creative energies uninhibited" is why the modern world is so much more prosperous, healthier—just plain *better*—than at any other time in history, you'll still find a lot of people inventing new and exciting ways of inhibiting them. You can't buy Scott's shoelaces for a couple of bucks because of central planning or taxation or regulation. They exist, like every other thing we buy, because millions of people—farmers, engineers, truckers, miners, and everyone else—are free to communicate their wants and needs to one another and to respond to them in the most efficient and inventive ways they can devise.

That's the real magic of free markets.

CHAPTER 5

December 2009: *WALL-E*-conomics

December 2009 is best remembered in the Kernen household for Blake's tenth birthday and the opening of James Cameron's megahit movie Avatar. *Both events got us thinking about what you can learn about the free market by watching TV and movies. It isn't what you think.*

People who work in and write about the movie and TV business tend to refer to it as the Industry—capital "I," if you please—which is pretty irritating, but not wrong. Filmed and televised entertainment generates more than $30 billion annually in the United States alone and is one of America's most profitable exports. Even those of us on the far outskirts of the world of *Dancing with the Stars* and *CSI* benefit from the enormous infrastructure—from the fiber-optic cable that transmits signals to the thousands of skilled craftspeople who capture images and sound on film or tape—created to compete for the attention of the country's 115 million households, both at home and in movie theaters.

Which is why the general attitude of the producers of filmed and televised entertainment toward business seems, to me anyway, mystifying. TV and movies don't just bite the hand that feeds them; they chew it into something that resembles hamburger.

This would be just a curiosity if it weren't for one thing: People believe what they watch. A recent study suggested that more than three-quarters of Americans get their primary information on business from television—and CNBC aside, TV isn't very happy with the way business is practiced. A survey of more than one hundred prime-time programs over the course of two seasons revealed, for example, that businesspeople commit four times as many crimes as gang members and five times as many as terrorists. Businesspeople committed as many murders and kidnappings as drug dealers, child molesters, and serial killers *combined*. I've met my share of ruthless businesspeople, but when I walk down a dark alley at night, I'd actually feel *less* nervous if I knew the sound of the footsteps behind me was being made by wingtips.

And I'd feel even better if I knew that Blake and Scott were immune to, or at least skeptical of, the way their favorite TV shows and movies treat the world of business. In order to know this, of course, I needed to find out what those favorite shows actually were, and for once, I didn't need to ask. I just had to check out the shows that had been saved onto our DVR.

"'iTake on Dingo'?"

"It's an episode from *iCarly*."

For the benefit of readers in families without young girls—and I hope you'll understand why I say you're only living half a life—I should explain that *iCarly* is a cable sitcom in which the show's main character, a teenager named Carly Shay, produces and stars in her own Web show while refereeing disputes among her friends and coping with teachers, and her guardian, a twentysomething older brother. It is one of the most successful franchises on the Nickelodeon network, generating revenue not only from advertising but also from spin-offs, including books, videogames, iPhone apps, Web sites, music downloads, and DVDs.

In the "Dingo" episode that Blake had saved, Carly and her buddies learn that quite a few of the signature features of iCarly.com were turning up on a cable show called *Totally Ten* and head off to Hollywood to confront the show's writers about the theft. For viewers who miss the joke that the cable company carrying *Totally Ten* is called "The Dingo Channel," the show has a side plot involving the frozen head of Charles Dingo, the founder of Dingo Studios. When the kids finally talk their way into the *Totally Ten* writers' room—which contains a whiteboard headed "Things We Can Steal from iCarly"—they have the following exchange:

"You can't just take our ideas, change them a little bit, and then pretend they're yours."

"You said we could."

"No, we didn't. We'll sue you."

"This is the Dingo Channel. We have the money, the lawyers, and therefore the power to do anything we want."

Okay. It's just a sitcom. The private joke of one multibillion-dollar media conglomerate—Viacom, owner of Nickelodeon—tweaking another aside, is there anything especially bothersome about a teen sitcom showing Disney—oops, I mean Dingo—as a bully?

By itself, probably not. But in the world of television, it isn't by itself. It is one of the most reliable features of filmed entertainment that big business equals bad business—an unexamined but toxic assumption that is even more common in Hollywood than in the most Progressive public-policy think tank. In fact, on those rare occasions when TV and movies portray the world of commerce in a (relatively) positive manner, you can count on the subject being small business, which is *always* more virtuous than big business.

Consider, for example, the Disney-theme-park-turned-billion-dollar-movie-franchise known as *Pirates of the Caribbean*. Once upon a time, the villains in pirate movies were always either other pirates or naval vessels in the service of a corrupt governor. And indeed, those were the villains in the first (and best) of the *Pirates* movies. By the second, however, a bigger budget allowed for the addition of not only a vengeance-seeking former Royal Navy commodore and a ship full of fish men in the service of Davy Jones, but also a sea monster roughly the size of a supertanker. Given all that, who do you think was the movie's *real* villain?

A multinational corporation, that's who.

The world's first multinational, in fact: the British East India Company, which, for unexplained reasons, had relocated to the *West* Indies for the duration of *Pirates of the Caribbean: Dead Man's Chest*. Actually, though the reasons are unexplained, they're also pretty obvious. If you need a character that immediately screams out, "I am a villain beyond any chance of redemption," then the easiest way is to make him a CEO. In this case, his name is Lord Cutler Beckett, his many-times-stated obsession is eliminating all freedom from the world, and his pet phrase, generally used to explain why he has, yet again, violated a solemn agreement, is "It's just business."

Now, the East India Company has a lot to answer for, not least because, while it was a consistent advocate for free *trade*, its devotion to free *markets* was essentially nonexistent. Its competitive advantage was built on the domination of India at the point of a gun—a domination that was secured by using its army and police force to rule the subcontinent from 1757 to 1858. But the real reason that the creators of *Dead Man's Chest* used the company was that, well, that's what movies do, especially when their audience is mostly kids.

It's hard to say whether Cutler Beckett is a cause of the widespread distaste for large and successful firms or just another symptom. Probably both: The more we see how malevolent commerce is—especially when compared to occupations as virtuous as, for example, piracy—the clearer it becomes as a symbol for villainy. And symbols are important; with one hundred or so minutes to tell a story (or forty-six or so for an hour-long TV show), economy is important, and being able to communicate a character's status rapidly is a jewel beyond price.

Case in point: If you didn't already know that the worst kind of business executive—the *very* worst, worse even than senior executives employed by murdering multinationals—is one who cuts down trees, spend a few minutes with Mr. Potter, the CEO of the logging company that is foiled by the title character in *Dr. Doolittle 2.* Or Mr. Muckle, the CEO of the pancake-house chain who wants to build a restaurant on a vacant lot occupied by a family of owls in *Hoot.* In today's television and movies, a bulldozer is the equivalent of a Nazi uniform: a symbolic shortcut that screams, "Evil! Evil! Evil!" In a dramatic format that relies on conflict between good and evil, this saves a whole lot of expensive film.

And conflict is essential. Even someone like me, who never took an English or drama course that I could avoid, can understand why a story needs conflict. Not so obvious, though, is why the conflict so often takes the form of an underdog versus an overwhelming favorite—and why the underdog seems to have such a claim to the moral high ground.

I may not be a trained critic—okay, I am *definitely* not a trained critic—but I do know how to do research. And when I started researching this particular topic, I found that a lot of people had been there before me.

Many of them studied the place where the phenomenon appears most frequently: sports, where the need for a competitive contest practically obliges rooting for the team or player that is less likely to win. Sports fans, like ten-year-olds (and Progressives, especially those in positions of power), want everything to come out fair in the end, and the only way this could happen if, for example, the Yankees were to play my poor Cincinnati Reds, would be if the underdog were to overachieve.

There are other reasons. When they win, underdogs have a bigger return on emotional investment than favorites, who can only perform as expected or disappoint. This is also why, unaccountably, racetracks are full of people who underbid favorites and overinvest in losers.

Some of this is perception: In a sort of Lake Wobegon effect—where "all the children are above average"—more than six out of ten voters in the 2004 presidential election described their choice as the "underdog," and the same phenomenon caused them to see underdogs, in areas ranging from the Olympic Games to the Israeli-Palestinian conflict, as the ones who try harder. And who, after all, doesn't love the Little Engine That Could? By definition, 90 percent of people aren't in the top 10 percent in athletic ability, intelligence, wealth, or good looks, so if you want someone with whom an audience can identify, you're probably going to do a lot better with an underdog.

The underdog perspective is everywhere. It is the reason local news anchors can't finish a broadcast without a human-interest story about someone overcoming great odds. It's why they televise the hearings in which senators torment large and successful corporate executives. And it is especially the reason that business executives make such terrific villains.

Think I'm cherry-picking? Since it was first awarded in 2001, nine movies have won the Academy Award for Best Animated Feature (a tenth will have been awarded by the time you read this). Two of them—*Finding Nemo* and *Wallace & Gromit: The Curse of the Were-Rabbit*—have no real connection with, or attitude about, free enterprise, business, or the economy. Here are six of the others:

> *Shrek*: The villain, Lord Farquaad, is not only evil incarnate but also a monopoly capitalist bent on evicting all competing magical creatures from his kingdom, the Land of Duloc. The kingdom, by the way, is a totalitarian theme park obsessed with cleanliness, order, and enforced happiness—kind of like Disney's prototypical Magic Kingdom, against whom the CEO of DreamWorks, Shrek's studio, had a legendary vendetta.

Spirited Away: An anime movie that was, for a time, the biggest-grossing movie in Japanese history but went largely unseen in the United States (with just $10 million in gross receipts). Even so, the director's stated purpose was to show his distaste for modern Japan's habits of consumption. The main character's parents are credit-card junkies who are transformed into pigs, symbolism not very hard to follow.

The Incredibles: The hero—Bob Parr, Mr. Incredible—is forced to work as a customer supervisor at a health-insurance company, where his supervisor, Gilbert Huph ("Tell me how you're keeping Insuricare in the black! Tell me how that's *possible* with you writing checks to every Harry Hardluck and Sally Sobstory that gives you a phone call!") is a caricature of every corporate flunky who ever lived.

Happy Feet: Tacked on to a story about a dancing penguin yearning to escape captivity and return to his Antarctic home is a subplot about a rapacious fishing industry. The addition of a completely unrelated theme (overfishing = bad) results in a totally unnecessary second ending, but at least our kids get their dose of environmental anticapitalism to accompany the closing song.

Ratatouille: The plot for this movie about a young chef working in a three-star restaurant, inspired by the culinary talent of a rat, turns on the intentions of the restaurant's owner to link up with a multinational and—*Quel horreur!*—market a line of microwave burritos, barbecue, and corn dogs, therefore getting two for one: sneering not only at commerce but also at down-market American food. The ironic fact that the movie was shown in theaters serving hot dogs, popcorn, and nachos appears to have been lost on the filmmakers.

Up: Carl Fredricksen's house, in which he shared an idyllic life with his now-deceased wife, is targeted by a developer who buys all the land surrounding it, thus forcing Carl to (a) hit one of the construction laborers and (b) flee the scene of the crime by attaching a gazillion helium balloons to the house. Developer. Evil. 'Nuff said.

And then there's *WALL-E*.

Like most parents, I expect a *G* rating to stand for "generally harmless," as well as "generally boring." But this particular *G* was attached to a movie that was receiving the sort of reviews usually reserved for potential Oscar winners. And when we saw it at the multiplex in 2008, it was pretty impressive. On the screen, the camera's eye raced through the depths of interstellar space. Nebulae and galaxies flashed by. The members of the audience—several hundred parents and their children—watched patiently (parents) and eagerly (kids) as their destination came into view: Earth.

Or what was left of it, anyway. The scene was apocalyptic. Mountains of trash had replaced cities; high-tension towers and windmills were completely silent. The oceans had unaccountably dried up, the sky was the color of sewage, and not a single stalk of grass marred the perfectly sterile brownness. No plants. No animals. Well, one animal: a single cockroach. The lone sound was a snippet from an old movie musical played by the one purposeful thing on the entire planet. Earth was obviously dead—and as a rule of thumb, when the only sound heard for centuries is a song from *Hello Dolly*, you're not in heaven.

The cause was less obvious, at least until we rewatched the movie on DVD. Was it some unimaginably violent nuclear war? An attack by aliens out of some science-fiction nightmare? Could it have been a plague so deadly that not a single organism had survived? Or maybe some environmental catastrophe had been able to do what four billion years of asteroid strikes, earthquakes, and volcanic eruptions could not. What could have sterilized an entire planet?

Walmart.

Not literally Walmart. Not Walmart in a way that might expose the filmmakers to a cease-and-desist letter. The author of earth's destruction, according to Pixar and the creators of the movie *WALL-E* (or at least their attorneys), was the super-ultra-mega corporation known as Buy n Large, sometimes shortened to "BNL." Throughout the garbage heaps of the dead city in which *WALL-E* opens, the only recognizable trademark is that of Buy n Large. A Buy n Large Ultrastore, roughly the size of the Pentagon, stands empty in a vast parking lot. Buy n Large gas stations. BNL transit stations. Even the newspaper that is one of the millions of articles of trash filling the streets is a Buy n Large production. Earth has been destroyed not by fire or by ice but by Everyday Low Prices.

But more about that later. First, a confession. I liked *WALL-E*. Blake liked *WALL-E*. Pretty much everyone liked *WALL-E*. It's a good movie. The robot characters are funny, affecting, and memorable. The combination of pictures and sound without dialogue, particularly during the movie's first forty minutes or so, is terrific. The movie enjoyed both huge ticket sales and critical acclaim, and it earned both. Only a killjoy would see it primarily as anti–free market propaganda, and only a complete idiot would tell his daughter that he thought so.

I'm not a *complete* idiot, anyway.

But I did turn off the *WALL-E* DVD, as I often do after sitting through one of Hollywood's unbearably smug attacks on the world of commerce, scratching my head while wondering whether the entertainment industry's consistently villainous portrayals of business and businesspeople are the results of hypocrisy or ignorance. Do the creators of films that generate billions of dollars in profit not care or not know?

WALL-E, for those who never saw it, is set on a future Earth that had been so poisoned by human garbage that virtually the entire population boarded immense spaceships, built and operated by Buy n Large, in order to cruise around the galaxy while BNL's robots cleaned up the mess left behind. Seven hundred years later, Earth is still devoid of human, animal, or plant life, and only one lonely robot—a Waste Allocation Load Lifter, Earth-class, or WALL-E—is left to package the trash into cubes with no apparent purpose.

He finds that purpose when another robot arrives, dispatched from the *Axiom*, one of the BNL spaceships, to discover whether earth can support life. WALL-E and EVE (for "Extraterrestrial Vegetation Evaluator") court each other to the sound of Louis Armstrong singing "La Vie en Rose." Soon enough, EVE learns that WALL-E has discovered a single plant growing in a discarded refrigerator, at which point she returns to the *Axiom*, with WALL-E following. There we discover that the seven-hundred-year-long cruise has left the human passengers grossly obese, completely passive, and utterly dependent on the perfect service offered by the ship and its computers, which have been following the directive given to them by their BNL builders: Since earth was too toxic to support life, the *Axiom* must continue its cruise forever.

At least until WALL-E's arrival. With the spaceship's captain, whose reading about Earth has sharpened his curiosity (though not his wits: "Earth is AMAZING. These are called 'FARMS.' Humans put seeds in the ground, pour water on them, and they grow food, like PIZZA!"). WALL-E and EVE lead a revolt that ends when the *Axiom* accepts the plant as evidence that earth can now support life, and the ship returns to disgorge its passengers like the Ark after the flood. WALL-E, who has been nearly destroyed, is brought back to life by EVE, and the two robots, along with Earth, live happily ever after.

What could be wrong with all this? Along with dozens of irritants that bother only the irritable (How in the name of photosynthesis did the planet's single surviving plant germinate in a refrigerator with neither water nor light? What does the cockroach eat?) are two that seem specially designed to illustrate the dumbing down of American economic literacy.

First is the notion that free markets, when they are permitted to run amok, lead inevitably to a single supercorporation that not only will dominate all economic activity and control all forms of economic demand—when the *Axiom*'s computer decides that all passengers will change from wearing red to blue, compliance is immediate and enthusiastic—but will do so *for more than seven hundred years*. This is mind-numbingly wrong, both theoretically and empirically. The defining characteristic of free market capitalism is that *nothing* stays the same for seven hundred years. Or even seventy. Ask U.S. Steel. Or General Motors. Or even Walmart's spiritual predecessor, the Great Atlantic & Pacific Tea Company, which once upon a time controlled 80 percent of America's supermarket business. If free markets aren't dynamic, they aren't free; they need what the Austrian-born economist Joseph Schumpeter called "the perennial gale of creative destruction" to operate as productively as possible.

This doesn't mean there aren't any examples of economic stagnation. That's what describes almost all of human history, after all—before, that is, the advent of free-market capitalism. The same story applies to single enterprises dominating all economic life, which appeared in dozens of preindustrial civilizations and even some nations of the industrial age; a few of the mid-twentieth-century communist nations got fairly close. However, their experience reveals the second of *WALL-E*'s glaring misunderstandings of economic behavior. Even if you accept that, for historically mysterious reasons, a single corporation was able to eliminate all competition and all substitutes for the products it sold, it would *for that very reason* be unable to operate efficiently.

Try it this way: The *Axiom*'s "economy" is run on the principle that one supersmart computer can anticipate all the conceivable demands of hundreds of thousands of human consumers and satisfy them so well that those consumers get fat enough that they can barely move. This was the core myth of the twentieth century's command economies (to say nothing of the dreams of Progressivism), whose history should remind even the producers of animated films that the traditional result of central planning is not overindulgence but famine. This wasn't because the central planners lacked intelligence, digital or otherwise, but because they lacked information. If there are no competitors, the one remaining firm (or, as with true command economies, the government) gets no information about consumer demand in the form of the prices consumers are willing to pay.

Price mechanisms, or signals, are just another way of describing what happens when you shop for everything from detergent to houses: If you (and a thousand shoppers like you) choose to forgo the new-and-improved good-for-the-environment laundry soap at $10 a bottle in favor of the old-fashioned one at $5 a bottle, manufacturers lower the price or stop producing it at all. Sooner or later, supply and demand are brought into balance—a *temporary* balance, since shoppers have a tendency to change their minds. But when the soap manufacturer, like some 1955 Soviet economic planner, has to make decisions about what to make and how much to invest with no market information at all—well, if there is a lesson from the Soviet Union's five-year plans, it is this: Consumers in such a system don't get fat and lazy because all their needs are met.

And yet that is the world of *WALL-E*. Everyone on the *Axiom*— and, I guess, everyone on the earth they fled—lives in a world run by a computer that somehow meets all conceivable consumer demand without ever changing, without anyone working, without anyone ever even exhibiting the curiosity of a paramecium.

The overthrow of such a system is stirring, of course, even if its existence is unfathomable in any real-world economy. But once the humans onboard the *Axiom* do revolt and get rid of their computer rulers, their behavior is even weirder. For upon their return to Earth, what do they do?

They become farmers. Organic farmers, I suppose, though not of the most sophisticated variety. (The *Axiom*'s captain announces: "You kids are going to grow all kinds of plants. Vegetable plants. PIZZA plants!") Not only that, but as the end credits roll, *WALL-E*'s creators offer up a recapitulation of human history, beginning with the return of the *Axiom*. The newly returned humans plant seeds. They rediscover fire. In a credit sequence that is an homage to the Egypt of, say, 3000 BC, they discover wells. They learn how to cultivate wheat and grapes. Fish repopulate the oceans. Cities are rebuilt (using, of course, sustainable production materials and hand tools). The planet blooms. People lose weight. By the time the credits finish, humanity, which began the movie as spacefarers able to travel faster than the speed of light in an environment that had conquered starvation and disease, have finally progressed to, I think, the Middle Ages.

The natives of Pandora, the setting for James Cameron's *Avatar*, have so little use for technology of any sort that they make the *Axiom* look like an advertisement for the wonders of progress; *WALL-E*, after all, at least holds out the hope that technology can serve human aspirations. Pandora's Na'vi, not so much.

For readers who have been in a coma for the last two years, *Avatar* tells the story of a paraplegic Marine veteran, Jake Sully, who is recruited into a program intended to study the Pandoran natives— the blue-skinned, nine-foot-tall Na'vi—in order to improve the chances of negotiating mining rights. The object of those rights, named (don't laugh) "unobtainium,"* is vaguely but critically important for the continued survival of Earth, which, we are told, is on the brink of extinction because of some unnamed, but probably human-caused, environmental crisis. As the story begins, the humans'

---

* The term has actually been used by engineers for fifty years as shorthand for a material that is perfect for some use but doesn't exist, like a wire with no mass that conducts electricity with no resistance.

"avatars"—Na'vi bodies that are able to host the consciousness of human operators—have not succeeded in persuading the technologically primitive Na'vi to permit the mining operation, but humanity has a plan B: Take the needed land by force, using a battalion of high-tech mercenaries employed by the mining consortium and led by a colonel who closely resembles a half-starved pit bull, only less likable.

However, Jake (or more precisely, his avatar) goes native big time. Enchanted by the Na'vi ability to live in harmony with nature, and by a beautiful Na'vi princess, he leads his new people to an implausible victory over the rapacious miners, who are sent home to their dying planet. I mean, our dying planet.

The plot for the movie has no real surprises: Mining companies bad. Native Americans—oops, I mean Na'vi—good. Good defeats bad. It's all been done before, a dozen times (though not with such admittedly spectacular technical skill). In an animated movie titled *The Battle for Terra*, for example, the last remnant of humanity—led by a violent general—attempts to destroy a harmless native population and colonize its planet but are foiled by a human who betrays his species in support of the technologically primitive locals. Or for that matter, take Kevin Costner's Lieutenant Dunbar in *Dances with Wolves*, in which a U.S. cavalry officer leaves his own world for that of the Lakota Sioux. Even by comparison to its predecessors, however, the environmentalism that drives *Avatar* is especially pure, to the point that even the extinction of humanity seems an okay price to pay for the actual sin of despoiling Earth and the proposed sin of exploiting the mineral wealth of Pandora. One might think that the miners' motives—saving their planet—might make a difference, but it doesn't.

The really interesting thing about *Avatar*, however, is how it underlines the link, in popular culture, between hostility to free markets and a certain sort of environmentalism. Or more accurately, environmental romanticism.

Environmental romanticism is the belief that the natural world is just better than the human world (forgetting, for a moment, that humans are just as "natural" as rain forests). Nature is morally superior. It's more spiritual. And it's even better looking. Without *Homo sapiens*, the natural world would revert to a stable and unchanging perfection. If humans want to live in such a paradise, they have to be as inoffensive as possible. In fact, they have to be invisible.

Blake, whose ten-year-old heart has never found an animal or plant that it didn't want to save, is especially vulnerable to this kind of romantic view of nature. Whether hanging around at our local nature preserve or supporting animal rights, she is incapable of seeing environmentalism in anything but a good light. In the movies set on Pandora (or on Terra or in the Wyoming Territory) that light shines on a conflict between nature and technology, and when that happens, you can bet any amount of money that the nature in question is going to be beautiful, and—so long as it isn't attacked—beneficent. *Avatar* is simply the most successful version of this reliable theme, so successful that a sizable number of viewers were actually depressed after seeing the movie, repulsed by the world around them after seeing the incredibly beautiful and hospitable world of Pandora.

What makes Pandora so attractive, however, is not phosphorescent plants and beautiful "birds" (and gorgeous Na'vi princesses). What makes the Garden of Eden Edenic is that it doesn't change.

Of all the characteristics of the paradises described by every culture, that's the one constant. No one gets poorer or richer or older. In paradise—and as we learn at the end of *Avatar*, on Pandora—there's not even a need for anyone to die. It's like Peter Pan's Neverland: adventures galore, but the good guys never die. All is in balance. In this way, as in so many others, it is the exact opposite of a free market, which is both powered and steered by those famous "prerennial gale of creative destruction."

That destruction, of course, is what the Na'vi stand against, but there is another, more subtle, way in which *Avatar* is a perfect expression of economic muddleheadedness. And that is the reason for the story's conflict: the fact that Earth has run out of so many critical resources that the only solution is mining the magic stuff—the unobtainium—out of Pandora.

The most familiar theme in all of environmentalism is that we are *always* running out of stuff, usually the stuff most critical to industrial society. Environmentalists regularly discover shortages of everything from trees to biodiversity, but the most-repeated mantras have to do with fossil fuels. "Peak oil"—the idea that oil production has reached a peak, after which a decline is inevitable, which was first articulated by the geologist M. King Hubbert in the 1950s—has been followed, in rapid succession, by peak gold (a pretty impressive discovery, given the billions of ounces already in bars, Krugerrands, and wedding rings), peak lithium (a critical element in lithium-ion batteries), peak nitrogen, peak mercury, peak selenium, peak aluminum, peak phosphorus, peak copper, peak silver, and—wait for it—even peak helium, the second-most-abundant element in the universe.

This particular blind spot, of course, is why Paul Ehrlich lost that famous bet to Julian Simon back in 1990. But—as mentioned above—writing a $600 check didn't stop the doomsaying professor from continuing to preach that just about every commodity on which civilization depends was in permanent and irreversible decline.

The idea of decline almost demands opposition to free markets; it's a short leap from a belief in inevitable shortages to the idea that wealth acquisition is a zero-sum game—when someone gains, someone else must lose. Both are consequences of a belief that the pie is finite and every slice taken leaves one less for everyone else.

"Blake?"

"Yes, Dad?"

"How many slices of pizza do you want?"

"Two."

"Scott? How many for you?"

"Two."

With only three slices of pizza left, conflict loomed. We had passed the "peak pizza" point.

"Dad?"

"Yes, Blake?"

"I'll have one slice and a bagel."

Kernen nutritional habits aside,* Blake illustrates a principle that somehow seems to elude environmentalists and moviemakers alike. And its elusiveness isn't because it's just been discovered (though I just did discover it, as part of writing this book); it's been around since 1890, when the legendary economist Alfred Marshall first described it, "for purposes of convenience, as the Principle of Substitution."

The substitution principle is actually fairly simple: The cost of producing anything can be divided into component parts that are combined in what economists (who can't stand simplicity) call "inputs for production functions." To maximize profits, or minimize cost, manufacturers constantly change the combination, substituting one input for another.

This is why we don't run out of stuff, even when there's a finite supply of it. It's not just what we saw in chapter 3: that in a free market, a commodity that gets more difficult to find or expensive to produce (or that becomes more in demand) sees its price rise, which increases the incentive to find more of it. It's that when the price rises enough, another commodity is substituted for it—a bagel for a slice of pizza, for example. Long before we run out of copper, we substitute fiber-optic cable for it. The Stone Age didn't end because we ran out of stones.

---

* For that, you'll have to read chapter 8.

The substitution principle is a key component of free markets and is therefore one of the most important of Schumpeter's winds. To those who romanticize the unchanging features of paradise, whether on Earth or on Pandora, the wind is about as welcome as a forest fire, but as even environmentalists recognize, fires are as necessary for a healthy ecosystem as rain and sun.

The entertainment "industry" has a lot of practice contributing to America's (and the world's) economic illiteracy. So much practice, in fact, you might figure that hostility to free markets is practically a requirement for successful moviemaking. If you want either commercial or critical success, or just want to persuade a studio to bankroll your latest project, you just *have* to be demonizing big business.

Or maybe not. Though there aren't very many movies and TV shows that depict business and free enterprise in a positive light, audiences and critics *have* flocked to those few that do. Martin Scorsese certainly made a hero out of Howard Hughes, fighting the crony capitalism that made PanAm a de facto government monopoly in *The Aviator*. The bookselling tycoon in *You've Got Mail* is wealthy, competitive, *and* sympathetic. (Well, he's played by Tom Hanks, so of course he's sympathetic.)

But those are movies aimed at adults. Exhibit A for the defense is one of Blake and Scott's favorites: Tim Burton's 2005 version of the Roald Dahl classic *Charlie and the Chocolate Factory*.

As the movie opens, Charlie Bucket is living in the most over-the-top poverty ever seen on-screen. His father is employed, if you can call it that, screwing the caps on toothpaste tubes by hand. His four grandparents spend their entire days in a single bed, complaining. Cabbage soup is all the family can afford to eat—and after Charlie's dad loses his job to a machine, not even that.

So when, against all odds, Charlie wins a trip to the legendary

Wonka chocolate factory, viewers will be forgiven if they expect the film to blame the enormously successful Willie Wonka for their troubles. But the movie does anything but. The movie's star, Johnny Depp as the chocolate tycoon Willie Wonka, is practically an encyclopedia of neurotic tics—can't bear to be touched, can't even say the word "parent"—but it's not too much to call him heroic. No Ayn Rand character better exemplifies the virtues of free-market capitalism. Wonka is the world's greatest chocolatier because he is more creative—ice cream that won't melt, a single candy that satisfies for an entire day—and harder working than his competitors. He is even more ruthless, though in a thoroughly honest way.

Most movie factories, ever since Charlie Chaplin's *Modern Times*, have been spirit-crushing places. In fact, this has been true ever since Charles Dickens, whose factories' machines are explicitly monstrous. Not Wonka's. His factory is an amusement park, with machines that may not be entirely safe—Charlie's companions on his trip discover that they bite—but are nothing if not fun. They are the perfect reflection of their creator's genius, and there is no point at which his success is shown as anything but well deserved.

And Charlie's dad, who lost his job at the toothpaste factory? Far from resenting the loss of the job he described as "hours long; pay terrible," by the end of the movie he has taken on a job repairing the machines that replaced him. "Things," we are told, "had never been better for the Bucket family." Nor had they ever been better for the filmmakers. Despite the lack of cheap shots at free markets, *Charlie and the Chocolate Factory* was one of the biggest-grossing movies of the year; in inflation-adjusted dollars, it's still one of the hundred most successful movies of all time.

Which just reminds me that I still don't understand the reflexive hostility of the entertainment business to free markets and capitalism. Maybe the best explanation is that the writers, directors, and actors who produce our filmed entertainment are allowed (maybe even encouraged) to retain a child's view of the world. Like ten-year-olds, they retain a belief in obvious heroes and villains, in perfection as a place where things don't change (especially as the result of human action), and in happy endings.

Once again, just like Progressives.

CHAPTER 6

May 2010: America vs. Europe

On May 1, 2010—May Day—rioters armed with Molotov cocktails squared off against police in the streets of Athens. Their grievances were, by American standards, a little peculiar.

Ever since the 1880s, May 1 has been celebrated—if that's the word—as International Workers' Day. May Day (which I know has nothing to do with the distress signal, though maybe it should) has been uniting the workers of the world ever since the 1886 Haymarket Riot, a labor protest in which eight Chicago policemen were killed, and it has been a pretty rambunctious anniversary ever since, from the 1919 May Day riot in Cleveland, which ended with two dead and forty injured, to the Los Angeles "melee" of 2007 (twenty-nine marchers and a dozen police officers injured). In fact, the only places you can be sure that a riot *won't* occur on May Day are the few remaining traditional communist countries, where any temptation to get frisky in support of the proletarian cause is chilled out by battalions of tanks on parade.

Even so, Greece was, by May 2010, an extreme case. The simmering anger in Greece over the austerity measures needed to reform what was, at the time, the world's most fragile economy, had boiled over. After a year of protests against (among other things) the privatization of state-owned companies, changes in the law to make it easier to both hire and fire employees, and a decrease in government spending, the Greeks had had enough.

Two weeks earlier, a big chunk of America had also had enough and had been taking to the streets with protests of their own. And though those Tax Day protests were uniformly peaceful, the level of anger in Washington DC's Freedom Plaza on April 15 didn't look any different from what was going on in the streets of Athens.

There was, however, one pretty obvious difference between the two. The Tea Party protesters in the United States were demonstrating in *favor* of exactly the same things that the Greeks were *against*. The signs on view at the American demonstrations were demanding *more* austerity and *less* government. It's hard to imagine a bigger contrast between what we might call the European "street" and the American.

Now, I confess to a soft spot for the Tea Party activists. In fact, I sometimes feel the kind of proprietary feelings about the movement shared by people who saw the Beatles in Hamburg in 1962—or maybe more to the point, who were in the audience for Ronald Reagan's "A Time for Choosing" speech in support of Barry Goldwater's 1964 presidential campaign. You know, members of the there-at-the-beginning club. That's because on Thursday, February 19, 2009, I was in my usual spot at the anchor desk for *Squawk Box* while our manic reporter, Rick Santelli, was doing a live feed from the Chicago Mercantile Exchange. The economic news was, even by the standards of 2009, crappy. The TARP bailout had been passed some months earlier. The Obama administration, evidently embarrassed that the Bush White House had become the biggest spendthrifts in American history ("overspending is what *we* do"), had passed the $800 billion stimulus bill a few weeks earlier, and the previous day, the president had announced his "Homeowner Affordability and Stability Plan."

Santelli is not the quietest guy in the room at the calmest of times, but this morning I thought his head might explode. As he turned away from the camera to ask the floor traders which of them wanted to pay for their neighbor's mortgage, I told him, "They're putty in your hands." I was being sarcastic, but Rick evidently regarded it as a challenge and replied, "We're thinking of having a Chicago Tea Party in July."

The most distinctively American protest movement of the last century had been born. And by "distinctively American" I mean "distinct from Europe."

Now, don't start assuming that the Kernens are a bunch of unsophisticated rubes who, if they travel outside the United States at all, behave obnoxiously, speak English loudly and slowly to the locals, and in general behave like the prototypical "ugly Americans."* We love Europe. We had a great family vacation in 2008 in Portugal. We'll be going to Europe again and again as Blake and Scott get older.

But it's one thing to enjoy Paris or Lisbon or Rome as a vacation spot and a whole different thing to want to import European ideas into the American economy. It's easy to make fun of the Tea Party activists when they accuse the current administration of wanting to turn the United States into France, but it seems to me that they're on to something: A big part of the Democratic Party's agenda seems awfully comfortable with the European way of doing things and awfully *un*comfortable defending the American way.

"Blake, have you ever heard the phrase "'the American way'"?
"I think so."

---

* Although I still think the best travel book ever written is Mark Twain's *Innocents Abroad*, in which he famously complains about having Michelangelo (he calls him Michael Angelo) for breakfast, lunch, dinner, and between meals, finally admitting that he "never felt so fervently thankful, so soothed, so tranquil, so filled with a blessed peace, as I did yesterday when I learned that Michael Angelo was dead."

"In school."

"Not really so much."

Blake's teachers are uncomfortable even *describing* the American way, much less defending it. I'm guessing this is because there's so much negativity in the air about the subject, whether it's about exporting American ideals to other countries or even the idea that the American way of doing things might actually be superior. After members of the news media spent eight years criticizing George W. Bush for ignoring European leaders, they fell all over themselves to praise Barack Obama for cozying up with them. Europe, we are constantly told—or we *were*, before the Eurozone started having to spend hundreds of billions to support its weakest members—has figured out how to have a prosperous society that has practically vanquished inequality and where health care and education are not only better but cheaper. To a lot of these people, Ronald Reagan's belief in America as a "shining city on a hill" has become a punch line.

Not, however, in the Kernen household. I'm not so sure that the world is divided into America and Everyone Else, but I do believe that there *are* two different ways of seeing the economic world, and one of them is definitely more popular in the United States.

Actually, this idea is pretty widely held, both by people (like the Kernens) who think the American way is superior and by the trainloads of Progressives, liberals, and—of course—Europeans who think the American way is barbaric. Any time I find myself in agreement with so many people, it's a good idea to check my assumptions. Are America and Europe really all that different?

While I was checking those assumptions a few months ago, I came across a book by Peter Baldwin, a historian at UCLA, entitled *The Narcissism of Minor Differences: How America and Europe Are Alike*. As he points out, the measurable differences between modern Europe and present-day America are actually pretty small, smaller, in fact, than the differences between Spain and Germany or Iowa and California. A few of his observations:

- U.S. taxes are at least as progressive as European ones.
- Germans are even more litigious than Americans.
- Italians watch just as much TV (and just as much really bad TV) as Americans.
- The Swiss, Germans, French, and even Italians own more passenger cars per capita than Americans.
- The richest 1 percent of Americans owned about 21 percent of all wealth in 2000—exactly the same as in Sweden (and much less than Switzerland's 35 percent).
- Sweden, Belgium, and the Netherlands all have a higher percentage of poor citizens than the United States (poor defined as 60 percent or less of median income).

Some of these points are just handy to have around when some Frenchman or Swede looks down his nose at our unsophisticated ways, such as when they sneer about our dependence on cars for transportation as opposed to the better-for-the-environment-and-morally-superior high-speed trains used to travel across Europe. (It turns out that America transports ten times the amount of freight by rail that Europe does, which means that French families may get to the supermarket by train, but the stuff they buy there was transported all the way across country by trucks).

A lot of these similarities, though—and the better-known differences, such as the European "advantage" in education and health care—hide something pretty dramatic: The European economies have spent the last five decades benefiting from a giant free ride paid for by American taxpayers and consumers.

Start with defense. The U.S. Department of Defense spends three times as much as all of Europe, and what we're buying with all that money—$630 billion a year—doesn't just defend America. Ever since World War II, the United States has been responsible for the peace and freedom of Europe as well, and when three hundred million Americans are paying for the security of four hundred million Europeans, it frees up a huge amount of money for Europe to spend in other places: like welfare, or "free" health care.

Europe gets a free (or at least discounted) ride on health care as well. It's true that the United States spends more on health care than a typical European country without getting much better results—this was one of the arguments made on behalf of Obamacare. But one of the biggest reasons that health care is so expensive in the United States is the cost of drugs, which is a direct consequence of the fact that the United States is the only large economy where patent drugs are priced by the free market; in Europe and everywhere else, prices are controlled, or profits, or both. Thus, while the average American family actually takes fewer prescription drugs—only about three-quarters of the number taken in Europe—it spends nearly 40 percent more for the privilege. The United States is, literally, subsidizing the consumption of drugs all over the world—drugs that would never exist without a U.S. market that is willing and able to pay the roughly $800 million it takes to research and design a new drug.

The same thing is true of America's colleges and universities, where the basic research on so many of those drugs—and a lot of everything else needed by a technological society—originates. The professors I worked under at the MIT Center for Cancer Research in the late 1970s were the beneficiaries of a U.S. system that—precisely because it is partially private—spends nearly three times as much per capita on postsecondary education as any country in Europe and creates research and knowledge from which the whole world benefits.

"Blake, do you know what welfare is?"
"That's when you can't work."

"Right. Do you know who pays people who can't work?"

"I don't know; the government? Generous people?"

Somewhere along the way, it became standard editorial-page "truth" that America was a harsh place—one that might be wealthy but was stingy when it came to taking care of the poor. But the idea that the United States is less generous on social welfare turns out to be, well, ungenerous. Though Sweden (to pick what looks like a *really* generous European welfare system) spends 37 percent of its annual GDP on welfare, while the United States kicks in only a tightfisted 17 percent, these numbers are based on *gross* payments. Since the United States, unlike Sweden, typically collects no—or very little—tax on its payments, a calculation of *net* payments reduces the Swedish percentage of GDP to 29 percent, while the U.S. number rises to 19 percent. And it doesn't stop there: Since the United States is a whole lot more productive than Sweden, the right way to compare the numbers isn't as a percentage of the total economy but as a percentage of the population. After that little calculation, the differences almost disappear: Sweden spends $6,300 a year per capita (in 1990 U.S. dollars) while the United States spends $5,400—more, for example, than France, Germany, or Denmark.

And let's not forget the American private sector, not that I ever would: With net private social-welfare numbers added in, the United States takes over the lead, with $7,800 annually, 16 percent *more* than Sweden. Yes, Sweden. And here's the *really* impressive part: Even after absorbing the cost of providing the entire world with security, scientific knowledge, and miracle drugs, the American economy *still* blows everyone else out of the water. It's been doing so for quite a while, and it's still doing so today.

In the twenty-five years from 1980 to 2005, the per capita GDP in the United States grew at a rate 55 percent faster than it did in Germany and 48 percent faster than in France. Even after spending fifty years catching up after the Second World War, Germany's per capita GDP was barely 74 percent of the United States's and France's 72 percent. The reasons aren't very hard to see, since per capita GDP is nothing but the percentage of people with jobs, the annual hours those people worked, and the productivity of those hours: how much output per hour worked.

	Hours Worked in 2009	GDP per Hour Worked
United States	1,776	$38.00
Germany	1,309	$29.14
France	1,469	$35.74
UK	1,638	$29.51

Which means that the average American worker, *during the worst recession in seventy years,* put in more than 35 percent more hours yearly than the average German worker—and produced 30 percent *more* per hour in actual value.

The American economy is different, all right. But if the difference were just due to the free ride that Europe (and the whole world) has been taking on America's investments in stealth bombers and lifesaving drugs, then the difference would be only about sixty years old or so, because up until the end of the Second World War, European and American economic attitudes were pretty similar.

Which is what I thought when this project started. They're not. What I learned is that an even bigger reason that the social-welfare state is so much more entrenched in Europe than in the United States is simply that it had such a big head start: Fifty years before the New Deal, Germany was offering national health insurance—and by 1889, state-funded pensions. The situation faced by the German chancellor Otto von Bismarck even resembled the one that greeted Franklin Roosevelt when he took office in 1933. Like the 1930s, the 1870s were a time of worldwide economic depression, and one of the few growth industries during depressions is political socialism. The aristocratic Bismarck had little love for free-market capitalists but even less for socialists, and his first response was to outlaw socialist parties. But it was his second response that was the real success: in German, *Staatssozialismus*, which translates into English as "nanny state" (okay, really it's "state socialism," but it amounts to the same thing).*

The result was predictable. When you build a nanny state, you turn a decent-sized chunk of the populace into the sort of people who depend on nannies: infants. Or at least into the ten-year-olds who make the best Progressives and liberals. The whole German—and, soon enough, European—experiment in social welfare was based on the cultivation of people who believed their lives were determined by forces they couldn't control. The governments of Europe (and eventually the Labour governments of Great Britain) were, from the end of the nineteenth century on, committed to fostering a culture of dependency.

They didn't do it out of benevolence, either. The most important reason for building these European nanny states was to keep the locals from turning into revolutionaries, but Bismarck and his followers had another objective, too. All of those goodies given to Germans, in particular, were also designed to counter the dramatic emigration of Germans to the United States. Bismarck's government even made a point of publicizing the fact that, while wages (and opportunities) may have been greater in the United States, the value of those "indirect wages" (i.e., social insurance) should persuade many to stay home.

---

* You start trying to teach your children and end up learning a lot yourself. One thing I learned about was a man named Eugen Richter, a man who spent his life supporting free markets and trade and opposing both Germany's socialists *and* Chancellor Bismarck. Richter wrote a book titled *Pictures of the Socialistic Future*, in which he parodied—sort of—the kind of welfare state in which emigration is prohibited, since "persons who owe their education and training to the State cannot be accorded the right to emigrate, so long as they are of an age when they are obliged to work." Which doesn't say much about the United States but is a pretty good description of, oh, say, East Germany.

It succeeded—not only in reducing the rate of emigration but also in selecting the most docile people in Germany to stay and encouraging the least docile to go.

By then, European immigration to the New World was entering its fifth century; America was a nation of immigrants long before Americans decided that the "course of human events" forced them to wave good-bye to Mother England. And we've always been a little ambivalent about it. Immigration is such a thorny issue these days, particularly among conservatives, that I get a little twitchy just thinking about it. When I hear someone arguing that we shouldn't penalize the millions of immigrants who followed the rules about moving to the United States (and the millions more who are waiting at the borders for their paperwork to be reviewed) by granting amnesty to those who are here illegally, I find myself agreeing. And when I hear someone else saying that we can't expel eleven million people who are here illegally, I find myself agreeing with *that*. When one senator says we should reconsider the principle that everyone born in the United States is automatically a citizen, even if their parents came here illegally, I nod my head. When another one points out that we shouldn't amend the Fourteenth Amendment over this, I agree with that, too.

I'm an agreeable guy.

But there's one aspect of the whole mess I'm sure about. If you want to raise a population rich in the attitudes that start them off believing they are in control of their lives, rather than victims, then you want to encourage immigration. Legal immigration, of course, but immigration—and lots of it.

Wherever you find them, immigrants are the most income-mobile segment of society, partly because they start out at the bottom. But they don't stay there, at least not in the United States. After a typical immigrant household has been living here for one decade, its income is typically a third less than that of a native household. But after two decades, they're only earning about a fifth less—and after three decades only about 6 percent less. If they've become naturalized citizens in the intervening years, there's essentially no difference in income.

Immigrants are income mobile, but Americans are just plain mobile, at least compared to Europeans. In Germany, for example, barely 1.4 percent of the population moves from one "state" to another annually. In the United States, the number is nearly twice as high—and the real difference in mobility is much greater than that when you remember that Germany's sixteen states cover fewer square miles than California.

You see the same phenomenon when you look at the difference in the relative ease with which small businesses are formed in America versus Europe. The one-time costs of setting up a new business in the United States run a typical entrepreneur a little less than 2 percent of annual per capita income: approximately $1,000. In France that number is more than ten times greater: more than 35 percent of per capita income. As a result, not only does Europe produce a whole lot fewer entrepreneurial businesses—Germany produces 36 percent fewer start-ups as a percentage of existing businesses than the United States—but existing businesses hang on a lot longer: For every hundred businesses that vanish in the United States, only sixty-three go out of business in Germany. To a typical Progressive, this is a good thing, but it really just reflects far less of the creative destruction that is utterly necessary for free markets.

I'm not sure whether European statism produces economic stasis or if it's the other way around, but I'm absolutely certain that they go together. So if you're scared that team Obama is a little too eager to turn America into a European-style social democracy, you should be.

Every year, the Heritage Foundation publishes an index to economic freedom around the world. The index compares ten different aspects of each nation's economy—including tax rates, government spending, the ease with which new businesses can be started, the freedom to hire and fire workers, how well property rights are enforced, and levels of corruption—on a scale of one to one hundred and averages them to come up with a total score. Okay, it's more than a little wonky, but it's also useful.

It turns out that not all of the components measured are really strong indicators of economic success. The top scores in "fiscal freedom" (the taxes paid by individuals and businesses) include countries like Oman, the Maldives, and the Kyrgyz Republic; two of the "best" countries in the category of government spending are Burma and Turkmenistan. However, the top performers in other categories, such as trade freedom and property rights, are also the most free and most productive economies in the world: Western European countries such as France and Germany; English-speaking countries (Canada, Australia, New Zealand, and the United States), Japan, Hong Kong, and Singapore.*

One result is that on most of the measures of economic freedom that matter, the world's rich countries are hard to tell apart: Germany, Japan, and the United States all enforce property rights, are generally free of corruption, and permit the free flow of capital.

However, there is one measure on which they are wildly different—and it's the one that not only explains the differences in economic performance but also is a clue to its source. It's the category called labor freedom.

Labor freedom is the result of an equation that includes six different values: the ratio of the minimum wage to the average value added per worker, legal hindrances to hiring new workers, the flexibility in the number of hours an employer can ask an employee to work, the difficulty of firing employees, and how much notice and severance are required to do so (I told you it was wonky). The world's top three countries in labor freedom are Singapore, Australia, and the United States, all scoring at least ninety-four out of one hundred. In

---

* China and India are giant economic powers, but mostly because of their giant populations. China's per-capita GDP is essentially the same as Angola's; India's is less than Mongolia's.

the same category, France scores a 54.7 and Germany less than 40. (A different study, performed by the Organisation for Economic Co-operation and Development—OECD—in 1999, found that the countries with the strongest employment protections were Italy, Greece, Turkey, and Portugal. The weakest were the United States, the UK, New Zealand, and Canada.)

The European "way" in labor relations has some appeal, of course:

"Blake?"

"Yes, Daddy?"

"Do you know how many days there are in a year?"

"Three hundred and sixty-five." Eyes roll. "Dad, I *am* in fifth grade."

"And do you know how many of them most grown-ups get for their vacations?"

"Fifty?"

The average number of vacation days offered to workers in the United States is about thirteen. The minimum available to workers in the European Community is twenty, and the average is anywhere from thirty-five (in Germany) to forty-four (in Italy). But generous vacations are only the beginning. In Germany, for example, firing someone isn't just a months-long proposition: it's also like playing croquet with a flamingo in Lewis Carroll's *Alice in Wonderland*: Just when you get the head down, the bird's leg shoots up and the hedge-hog you're trying to hit runs away. At German businesses with a "works council," no one can be fired without consulting the council. Laws regulate how many hours employees are permitted to work and how many days they must take off. Other laws include the Commercial Transfer of Employees Act, the Act on Payment of Wages and Salaries on Public Holidays, and (my favorite) the Protection Against Dismissals Act, which, among other things, requires German employers to give employees at least four weeks' notice—and for workers with more than ten years on the job, four *months*—before firing them; to consult with the local works council on all dismissals; and if the fired worker challenges his or her dismissal, to appear in Labor Court to show that the firing was "socially necessary."

Sometimes it's hard to tell which management decisions are "socially necessary," but in Europe, managers don't have to make them alone; they have some of the most powerful unions in the world eager to help. In a number of European countries, a collective wage agreement negotiated by employers and unions is applied by law to everyone in the same business—which means that even a company that didn't negotiate the contract is bound by it. German courts even hold that employees are forbidden from taking wages lower than the collective bargaining agreement requires, whether or not they are union members or even whether their employers are signatories to the agreement. In Italy, everyone employed by a company with more than eighteen workers has the equivalent of tenure. One European trade union official is even on record saying that "workers who can afford to do so should work less." (He also seems to have some special hostility to the United States, where, in his words, "employees need three or four jobs to feed themselves." This is actually pretty funny given that Americans work fewer hours to buy more food than anyone in history—and especially funny when you think how Europeans love sneering at American ignorance about the rest of the world.)

The basic principle that defines work in Europe (and, all too frequently, in more Progressive parts of America) is that workers need to be protected against their employers. By building an entire economy on these lines, European economies have accepted that the only thing that keeps the average laborer from becoming a victim is the power of the state.

This culture of worker victimology has been a whole lot more popular in Europe than in the United States, so far, anyway. That's a big chunk of what those Tea Party protests are about: a distaste on the part of millions of Americans for seeing themselves as in need of government handouts. In this, as in so many ways, America's core beliefs about work, independence, and free markets are different from Europe's.

I started to understand one reason why the United States has a set of core beliefs about the economy (and a whole lot else) that is different from most of Europe when I read an article by the libertarian writer Lee Harris in which he points out that our most basic beliefs aren't things that we choose—not with our brains, anyway. Ideas about the world don't form our attitudes; our attitudes form our ideas. He explains this in terms of a fifty-year-old psychological theory that people tend to be divided into two basic groups: one whose "locus of control" is inside them and one whose locus is outside. "Internals" believe that they are in control of their own lives, while "externals" see themselves as subject to outside forces that they can't control. It doesn't matter much whether those forces are other people or luck or the impersonal laws of history: Externals view themselves as acted upon, internals as acting.

You can see where this is going, I hope. Free-market libertarians are internals. Social-welfare collectivists are externals. And for historical reasons, European nations have cultivated an "external" attitude that produces the sort of generous state welfare benefits that get the citizens of Athens (or Dublin or London or Paris or Madrid or Rome) to take to the streets whenever they are threatened.

But don't take my word for it. In 2006, the Pew Research Center Global Attitudes Survey revealed that Americans are twice as likely as Europeans to credit their success to their own efforts; they are *three times* more likely than even the legendarily hardworking Germans to say that children should be told that hard work is essential to that success. Three years earlier, in the same survey, 68 percent of Germans surveyed said that personal success is determined by forces outside their own control (up from 59 percent in 1991). The number in the United States? Less than 35 percent.

I guess it's not that surprising that a nation of *im*migrants would have stronger beliefs in aspiration, willpower, and individualism than a country of *em*igrants. You can see the effect in any number of economic statistics, but the strongest is one of the most powerful drivers of economic growth: starting up new businesses.

For the last ten years, a group of researchers at the London School of Economics and Babson College in Massachusetts have been running a program called the Global Entrepreneurship Monitor. It studies the way entrepreneurs thrive (or not) in more than fifty countries around the world, and one of its most consistent findings is that the factor that is most important in building an entrepreneurial economy is the degree to which the nation welcomes immigrants.

A big reason is the way immigrants view risk. After all, everyone knows that small businesses, from dry cleaners to restaurants, are pretty risky propositions (this is one of those things that "everyone knows" that turns out to be true). Almost by definition, immigrants are less risk averse than almost any other part of the population, and year after year the Global Entrepreneurship Monitor has found that those countries with large immigrant populations *always* have an edge in the annual number of business start-ups.

That's not true just in the United States but also elsewhere. In fact, it's even *truer* in the most immigrant-friendly nation in the world: Israel.

I can date the beginning of my interest in—and admiration for—Israel's economy pretty accurately. In September 2000, Penelope and I were flying home from a trip to San Diego with Blake, who was then only nine months old, and found ourselves on the same flight as Israel's former (and now current) prime minister, Benjamin Netanyahu. He was between jobs—he'd been prime minister from 1996 to 1999, but was, at the time, retired from politics, temporarily, as it turned out—but was still one of the most identifiable Israelis in the world.

My first reaction when I noticed him was nervousness; this was

still a year before 9/11 but that didn't mean that any flight with someone like Netanyahu wasn't likely to be a pretty attractive target for
attack. My second reaction, minutes later, was the exact opposite:
This was probably the *safest* flight I would ever take.

Anyway, we introduced ourselves: Just two MIT graduates with,
as it turned out, similar ideas about free markets and such. Since one
of us—not me—was, and is, a natural politician, Blake found herself being held and kissed by the once and future prime minister of
Israel—and one of the real architects of the biggest economic miracles of the last fifty years.

In its brief history, Israel has actually experienced *two* economic
miracles, both of them fueled by immigration. The first one occurred
in the twenty years after the state's founding in 1948, when the population of Israel grew from 800,000 to nearly three million and its per
capita productivity climbed from about a quarter that of the United
States to about 60 percent. However, during these decades, Israel was
still a nominally socialist economy, and most of its growth was a
function of a very impoverished starting point.

The first miracle, predictably, ran out of fuel in the 1970s. It's
hard to remember now, but Israel lost an entire decade to low growth
and hyperinflation—the inflation rate was 111 percent in 1979, 133
percent in 1980, and 445 percent in 1984—almost entirely because
of heavy-handed government intervention in the economy. In Israel
during the late 1970s and 1980s, the national government literally set
the terms for every loan and debt instrument issued in the country.
The only private-sector loans being made were for projects approved
by government, which effectively controlled both wages and prices.

Which makes the current state of affairs in Israel's economy even
more miraculous. Beginning in 1990, Israel started to welcome another enormous group of immigrants, this time 800,000 citizens of
the former Soviet Union, which would be equivalent to the United
States opening its doors to forty million immigrants.

Now, Israel has *always* welcomed immigration. It's the basic reason for the state. And it has always benefited from the presence of immigrants. But in the 1990s, these new immigrants were arriving in a country that was, largely at the urging of Netanyahu, embracing free-market principles. Finance, industry, defense, and transportation were all being privatized as fast as the new prime minister—Netanyahu was elected in 1996—could sign the papers.

The result is there for anyone with eyes to see and a brain to reason (this, all by itself, may explain the hostility to Israel among so many Progressives). As my friend Dan Senor points out in his book, *Start-up Nation*, Israel now has the highest concentration of engineers and R & D spending in the world—and the highest density of start-ups: one new business for every 1,800 Israelis every year. Israel, with a population of 7 million, attracts as much venture capital annually as Germany and France—with 145 million people—*combined*. Through the last decade of the twentieth century and the first decade of the twenty-first, through war (with Lebanon in 1996) and worldwide economic crises, Israel's economy has continued to be the world's most immigrant friendly, its most entrepreneurial, and one of its fastest growing. Our onetime companion on the San Diego–to–New York flight is promising to make Israel one of the world's ten richest economies in the next ten years, and I wouldn't bet against him.

Israel's Russian immigrants aren't completely typical; they are, as a group, far more educated and technologically literate than most. But they are only a part of the Israeli story, which includes large numbers of new citizens from places like Ethiopia and Yemen, as well. Israel in the 1990s didn't have to seek only the best-educated immigrants to see the phenomenon in action, any more than the United States did in the 1900s. This is because immigrants are also, as a group, younger than native-born residents in just about every country, which make them not just more entrepreneurial (though it does) but also more future oriented. America's larger percentage of immigrants is the biggest reason that the median age in the United States is three years lower than it is in France—and *seven* years lower than in Germany.

Other things can be relied upon in members of a more aspirational, "internal" culture. For one thing, people are a *lot* more competitive. Italian textile mills and tailors may make the world's most beautiful $4,000 suits, but they do so by behaving like medieval guilds. In fact, they *are* medieval guilds, still known as *associazioni di categoria* (in Italy even babysitters have them). Carlo Altomonte, a Milanese economist, even admits, "There is no sense of what a market economy is in this country. What you see here is an incredible fear of competition." No surprise in a country that's been sending a high proportion of its most competitive citizens—its "internals"—to the United States for centuries.

Internals also push back at being told what to do; even when they act collectively, they prefer doing so voluntarily rather than in response to compulsion. Three centuries ago, the Frenchman Alexis de Tocqueville knew this, writing in *Democracy in America*, "Wherever at the head of some new undertaking you see the government in France, or a man of rank in England, in the United States you will be sure to find an association."

And internals are suspicious of elites, even their own. Americans—those Americans who understand their birthright of freedom, anyway—know enough to distrust people who know a lot but don't know what they don't know.

About five years ago, while flying to San Francisco, I noticed that one of my fellow travelers was Nobel Prize–winning economist and *New York Times* columnist Paul Krugman, the man who has never met a governmental intervention in the economy he didn't like. There he was, flying first class inside a machine that is one of the most remarkable technological marvels of all time, moving at six hundred miles per hour toward what was probably a chance to pick up a five-figure check for speaking to some group for less than an hour (in

1999 Krugman's fee for speeches was at least $20,000). And all I could think was "Why is this guy so down on capitalism and the free market?"

In his 1942 classic, *Capitalism, Socialism, and Democracy*, the émigré economist Joseph Schumpeter gave me a clue. In his preface, he admits, "I felt it my duty . . . to inflict upon the reader . . . my paradoxical conclusion: Capitalism is being killed by its achievements."

The achievement he had in mind was the creation of a permanent intellectual class: "One of the most important features of the later stages of capitalist civilization is the vigorous expansion of the educational apparatus and particularly of the facilities for higher education." And since "the man who has gone through a college or university easily becomes psychically unemployable in manual occupations without necessarily acquiring employability in, say, professional work . . . all those who are unemployed or unsatisfactorily employed or unemployable drift into the vocations in which standards are least definite. . . . They swell the host of intellectuals . . . whose numbers hence increase disproportionately. They enter it in a thoroughly discontented frame of mind. Discontent breeds resentment [and] righteous indignation about the wrongs of capitalism."

Schumpeter had a bird's-eye view of the phenomenon; his employer at the time he wrote these words was Harvard University's economics department, which is just about as elite as you get.*

And as much as ~~The People's Republic of Cambridge~~ Harvard dislikes American free-market capitalism, it loves the European welfare state even more. In fact, it is pretty telling that European elites are likely to be anti-American, while their American counterparts are almost guaranteed to be pro-Europe. Hostility to American ideas about the free market or capitalism is actually one thing that elites on

---

* It would be poetic justice of a sort if Paul Krugman had a Harvard pedigree, but his academic credentials come from Yale and MIT, and he now teaches at Princeton. Same difference.

both sides of the Atlantic share. And one thing that the Kernen family, no matter how much we enjoy visiting Europe, can't abide.

"Blake, how do you train a dog?"

"To do what?"

"Anything."

"Well, you reward him when he does something right, and you say no! when he does something wrong."

There's a pretty well-known psychology experiment in which dogs were given a series of electrical shocks, with some of them able to stop the shocks by pushing a button and others unable to. The ones who couldn't, in the words of the researchers, "learned helplessness." I'm usually skittish about any parenting ideas that come out of a university psychology department, but this one actually says something to Penelope and me. If you want to raise kids to fight for their rights, to believe that they will be able to determine their fates, and to have faith that the future is theirs—and we do—then you can't teach them to be helpless. That's what *any* nanny state is teaching, and it doesn't matter whether the nannies—the elites—have the best interests of the nursery at heart.

And America is not a nursery. In his farewell speech to the nation in April 1989, my political idol, Ronald Reagan, gave his vision of America as a "city on a hill . . . a tall proud city built on rocks stronger than oceans, wind-swept, God-blessed, and teeming with people of all kinds living in harmony and peace, a city with free ports that hummed with commerce and creativity, and if there had to be city walls, the walls had doors and the doors were open to anyone with the will and the heart to get here." Almost exactly twenty years later, in April 2009, President Obama said, "I believe in American exceptionalism, just as I suspect the Brits believe in British exceptionalism and the Greeks believe in Greek exceptionalism."

The contrast is dizzying. Someone once defined capitalism as what people do if you leave them alone, and it works pretty well as a description of the United States of America. The European Community (and America's Europe-envying Progressives) is what elites do if you leave them alone. That's what the Tea Partiers have against the age of Obama. Me, too.

CHAPTER 7

June 2010: 99.985 Percent Pure:
The Price of Regulation

In June 2010, the Kernen family went to see a game played by the Cincinnati Reds at the team's home on the banks of the Ohio River. The Great American Ballpark, as it is known, is a replacement for Riverfront Stadium, which was a replacement for Crosley Field, which was part of the deal for keeping the Reds in Cincinnati in the 1960s—and if you think my free-market principles are in conflict with the way public funds were spent on a baseball stadium, I can only say: Get over it. Baseball is baseball.

It's also a good place to start thinking about the costs of regulation.

The Cincinnati Reds are my hometown baseball team, and I have been a fan as long as I can remember. The first World Series I remember was the 1961 Reds-versus-Yankees disappointment, which was nothing compared to the disaster of trading Frank Robinson for Milt Pappas (and the immortal Jack Baldschun) when I was nine. I grew up with Jim Maloney and Pete Rose and Tony Perez and Lee May and sweated out the threatened move to San Diego in 1967. And of course I firmly believe that the Big Red Machine of the mid-1970s was the greatest team ever. In fact, I feel sorry for anyone who doesn't realize this.

I'm aware that the years since haven't always been so glorious (and if I forget, my *Squawk Box* colleague Carl Quintanilla is always happy to remind me how the Phillies swept Cincinnati in the 2010 Division Series, only to lose to the Giants in the League Championship Series, which was at least some comfort).

Getting tickets to see the Reds has generally been pretty easy: Johnny Bench, the Reds' Hall of Fame catcher, is an old friend. However, in 2008 a series of screwups (mine; I had asked for tickets for the game being played the following day) left us without tickets for a Pirates-Reds game and no choice but to visit the entrepreneurs strolling along what used to be called Main Street (and is now Joe Nuxhall Way) in order to pay three times face value for the seats.

A lot of people, even those who end up buying scalped tickets, find this unfair. Blake isn't one of them. She had no problem with paying a lot for the tickets, not because of what economists call price inelasticity—this is the phenomenon that keeps demand from falling for certain categories of stuff, even when their prices rise; we don't buy less Halloween candy just because the price goes up, not in the Kernen household, anyway—but because *her* cost for the tickets is the same whether we pay list price or five times list price: zero.

However, "price gouging" at sporting events, plays, and concerts is subject to a dizzying amount of regulation and prohibition. The last time anyone checked, twenty-six states and dozens of municipalities representing three-quarters of the U.S. population—and including virtually every city with an MLB, NFL, or NBA franchise—have some kind of antiscalping regulation. Ninety years ago such laws were sold to the public as, essentially, antinuisance laws, like a requirement to clean up after your dog. What happened was that one nuisance—scalpers cluttering the sidewalk in front of baseball stadiums and concert arenas—was replaced by an even bigger one: the inability to buy a ticket to the event. As always with good intentions, the results were nothing like the original intent.

Welcome to the wide and wonderful world of regulation.

The desire to regulate economic life might be *the* defining characteristic of Progressive philosophy. It combines a mistrust of the free market in allocating resources; an appeal to a vague and indefinable virtue ("fairness"); a desire to achieve perfection in economic outcomes; a deference to experts over the judgment of ordinary folks; and, best of all, a chance to tell other people what to do. Oh, heck, let's just say it: Regulation *is* progressivism.

It is also the perfect way to illustrate just how much Progressive thinking depends on treating adults like kids. Because kids *love* regulation.

"Blake?"

"Yes, Dad?"

"You know cigarettes are bad for you, right?"

Eyes roll upward.

"And you know that people aren't allowed to smoke in restaurants or lots of other places, right?"

"They shouldn't be allowed to smoke *anywhere*."

"Why not?"

"Because it's *bad*!"

The usual argument offered by Progressives who want to ban indoor smoking is that secondhand smoke is so dangerous that it presents a clear and present danger to nonsmokers as well. Then, when restaurants and bars proposed segregating smokers and nonsmokers, the Progressive response was to leap to the defense of bartenders and waiters, who presumably had no choice but to work in places that permitted a tinge of tobacco smoke. New York City is currently considering banning smoking in the new "pedestrian islands" in Midtown streets that have been partly blocked from automobile traffic, evidently so that nonsmokers can safely sip their drinks without any tobacco smoke added to the exhaust of a thousand cabs and buses.

Ninety years ago, reform-minded Progressives wouldn't have felt any need to hide their real reasons any more than Blake did: The logic behind the movement to prohibit alcohol consumption by amending the Constitution—a movement led by Progressives—was simply that people need to be forbidden things that are bad for them.

Unfortunately, it's hard to know when to stop.

"What about McDonald's, Blake?"

"What about it?"

"You know that fast-food burgers aren't real good for people either, right?"

"So?"

"So . . . should people be allowed to eat food that's bad for them?"

Blake thought about this for a minute.

"I have it: People who are fat shouldn't be allowed to go to McDonald's."

"You want to put a scale in every fast-food restaurant?"

"Uh-huh. Though . . ."

"What?"

"Maybe if they weren't too fat, they could eat at McDonald's once a month."

In November 2010, the city of San Francisco did Blake one better: The city's board of supervisors voted to forbid any restaurant from giving away toys with "unhealthy" meals, thus protecting children from the peril of Happy Meals. What's unhealthy? Any meal of more than six hundred calories with more than 35 percent of them from fat (toys can still accompany meals below that threshold—so long as they have both fruits and vegetables as well). This is a reminder, if you really need one, that regulations get complicated really fast. They demand rules. Lots and lots of rules. Which is one of the reasons a regulatory response to pretty much anything is comforting to a ten-year-old: Blake's entire life—and Scott's—consists of rules: things that are either forbidden or required.

I'm just worried that we're headed into a future in which that will be true when they're adults, as well. Partly, this is because the Obama administration has the urge to regulate in its most virulent form. The Office of Information and Regulatory Affairs, under Obama nominee Cass Sunstein (according to conservative writer David Frum, who originally supported Sunstein's appointment), has approved literally hundreds of new mandates and prohibitions, including a ban on the sale of oysters in months without an *R* (actually just the summer, but you get the idea); regulation of the refrigeration temperature of eggs; and imposition of a $27,500 fine on airlines for every passenger stuck on the tarmac for more than three hours. No one has any idea how this number was arrived at, since even the lawyers who will be hired to fight the lawsuits that will be the regulation's inevitable result don't charge $9,167 dollars an hour.

This doesn't mean that all regulations, or even most, are intended to protect Americans from harm, or even inconvenience. For every construction building code that is required to guarantee that a new structure is (mostly) fire safe or that its plumbing won't spew raw sewage into a public catch basin, for every regulation that requires a restaurant to maintain a clean kitchen or a rancher to test cattle for disease, there are a dozen—probably a hundred—other regulations written to protect one group of Americans from another.

In the Obama era, the group that gets regulatory protection is, most often, a labor union.* But there are plenty of other folks who owe their prosperity to regulation. Not all crony regulations are national in scope or written to help out million-member unions. Just as ridiculous are the thousands of licensing laws written to protect, ahem, special interests.

Consider, for example, the tour guides who will be happy to show you where the First Family lives. You might think that the risk to public health of an unlicensed tour guide explaining when the Capi-

---

* For more on unionism, see chapter 9.

tol dome was constructed is minimal. But that doesn't stop the city of Washington, DC, from requiring that anyone doing so must have a special license costing a couple of hundred dollars in fees just for the application. And don't forget the test: a passing grade on the District of Columbia Sightseeing Tour Guide Professional Licensing Exam—so unless you know that the Smithsonian National Zoological Park (the "National Zoo") isn't technically a Smithsonian Museum but a Smithsonian Research Center, well, you're out of luck.

Don't plan on traveling to DC anytime soon? How about getting your hair cut? Cosmetology licenses—which can cost $15,000 to acquire, a big chunk of which is paid for by government-insured student loans—are usually justified on safety grounds: People who use razor blades or caustic chemicals around the face are easy targets for fearmongering. And thank the regulatory gods that someone makes sure that no one is going blind from having bleach sprayed into her eyes—except that the risk, once again, seems modest. The United Kingdom, which doesn't have a lot of hostility to regulation in general, doesn't require *any* license to cut or style hair and hasn't required one since 1964—without, so far as I can tell, any epidemic in infection, hair loss, or lost ears.

One reason that licenses are so pervasive is that states and municipalities make money issuing them (as do the schools and trainers who make a living preparing people to take the tests required to earn them). But the real support for such licenses, inevitably, comes from the people who have them and are understandably peeved at the prospect of competitors who haven't spent the same amount of time and money to join the club. As Matthew Yglesias points out, on the South Side of Chicago, where a significant number of African American women like their hair braided, licensed cosmetologists got in the habit of calling in the police to raid the shops of hair braiders, who learned their skill as apprentices because most cosmetology schools don't even teach it.

The Institute for Justice, based in Arlington, Virginia, documents hundreds of similar licensing scams, which make for entertaining reading so long as you can forget their economic costs. If you want to be a used-book seller in the city of Los Angeles, for example, you may be required not only to get a police permit but also to fingerprint a customer trying to sell you a collection. The District of Columbia protects not only tourists from unlicensed tour guides but also home-owners from interior designers who have failed to pass a thirteen-hour test. And it isn't just Chicago looking out for barbershop customers: In Newark, New Jersey, cutting hair means working for a fully licensed barber for three years before doing it on your own.

Anytime the government regulates entry to a profession, the re-sult is protectionist, no matter what the original impulse, and the people who are protected tend to like it that way. New York City, for example, forbids any cab without a license—a "medallion"—from picking up passengers at airports or on streets, and because the city didn't issue a new medallion for more than fifty years, the only way to get one was to buy one from an existing owner, at a cost that even tually reached several hundred thousand dollars—ten times the cost of the cab itself. Not very surprising, then, that medallion owners *love* that particular regulation—or that tens of thousands of New Yorkers can't find a cab during rush hour.

Licensing regulations, no matter how obviously they benefit one group at the expense of everyone else, are usually sold to the public as a public benefit: more safety or reliability or something. Other regu-lations are sold to the public to correct a "failure of the market."

That phrase, of course, is a loud warning siren for anyone who believes in the free market, since the idea that the market can't pro-duce what some people think of as an efficient (or, more likely, "fair") outcome is one of the first commandments of Progressivism. The typical regulation-happy Progressive, for example, *always* argues that laws are needed to regulate industries that are "natural" monopolies, like telephone service or power utilities. The market, they tell us, can't allocate these "scarce" resources; without regulation of telephones and electric power, the argument goes, companies would build a dozen telephone poles outside every house in America.

The reality, as always, is a little different. Way back in 1960, an economist named Ronald Coase took on the idea of the need for government regulation in the free market, even in those areas where everyone "knew" the need was obvious. Radio airwaves, for example, "needed" regulation because otherwise stations would broadcast on frequencies that were too close together, thus interfering with clear transmission. Coase showed that so long as there were clear property rights to given frequencies and low costs for buying or selling those rights, the market would very quickly resolve any interference problem, since the station that wanted the space in the broadcast spectrum more would pay the station that wanted it less.

Needless to say, this is not exactly a communications policy favored by Progressives—in this case, generations of Progressives in both political parties—who fear and distrust *any* solution that is generated by the unaided free market. But whether the stated reason for regulation is public safety, promotion of a "good" special interest (like unions or homeowners or the disabled), or prevention of "market failures," the most reliable characteristic of regulations, in addition to adding cost to economic transactions—something that Progressive bureaucrats aren't paid to care about anyway—is that they hardly ever accomplish what they were intended to do, and almost *always* have some genuinely bad unintended consequences.

For example, while I made fun of licensing barbers and tour guides above, the Kernen family actually likes hiring licensed plumbers and electricians because of the peace of mind that comes with the (sometimes naive) belief that the people installing a new toilet actually know what they're doing. Similarly, when I had an emergency appendectomy last year, I didn't check to see that the surgeon had actually attended medical school, trusting to the various regulations—board certifications, state licensing—that would do the checking for me.

However, that unseen diploma is actually a pretty good example of the problem with good regulatory intentions. Back in 1910—not at all coincidentally, the high point of the first American Progressives—the Carnegie Foundation hired a guy named Abraham Flexner to write a report about the state of American medical education, which was, at that moment, kind of a mess. America's medical schools were more like vocational schools, usually run by a few doctors and requiring nothing more of their students than a couple of years of lectures, with no lab work or hands-on practice. Most didn't even demand a high-school diploma. The Flexner report recommended a whole lot of changes: requiring at least two years—later four—of college, plus at least four years of medical education, plus additional time to learn a specialty. It also recommended closing the medical "trade schools"—reducing the number of medical schools from 155 to 31—and requiring every medical school to affiliate with a university.

The result, once the recommendations were adopted by the medical establishment—and, very important, enforced by state regulations—was a system of medical education that looks a lot like the one my surgeon went through. It also created a regulatory cartel. Since no medical school could open its doors without the approval of the state medical association (or educate more than a state-approved number of doctors), the number of physicians dropped like a stone, resulting in a *lot* more income for the ones left. And much larger medical bills for the American public. Better medical education was definitely a well-intended Progressive goal; its price was an agreement to not just improve medical education but also to restrict it in order to keep prices high.

Or consider the Americans with Disabilities Act. Hardly any federal legislation of the past fifty years had better intentions or more widespread support; in 1990 the ADA passed the U.S. House of Representatives by a vote of 377 to 28 and the Senate by a vote of 91 to 6. Its primary objective was to improve job prospects for disabled Americans. However, employment of disabled men in their prime earning years—age twenty-one to fifty-eight—*declined* after the passage of the ADA—almost certainly because the ADA turned the disabled into litigation time bombs, or at least created that perception in the minds of potential employers.

The ADA also produced at least one unintended consequence that deserves to be called mind-boggling: As reported by the invaluable libertarian reporter John Stossel, the *Exxon Valdez*'s captain, Joseph Hazelwood, had already been in rehab for alcoholism before running his tanker aground in Prince William Sound in 1989. In response, Exxon subsequently prohibited employees with a history of drugs or drinking problems from holding similar jobs. However, in the intervening months, the ADA had passed, with the result that those employees argued that alcoholism was a disability, then sued under the law's nondiscrimination provisions—and won.

Want more? The explosion of BP's Deepwater Horizon drilling rig on April 20, 2010, was by any measure a huge mess: nearly 5 million barrels (or 185 million gallons) of crude oil. For months the cleanup, which as of this writing is still going on, was priority number one for dozens of different federal, state, and municipal governments—or it should have been. A short list of even higher-ranking regulatory priorities would include the following:

- On June 18, sixteen oil-sucking barges were shut down by the Coast Guard, pending an investigation to make sure there were enough life preservers onboard (there were). "The Coast Guard is not going to compromise safety. . . . That's our number one priority," according to its spokesman, Robert Brassel.
- The 1920 Jones Act—a naked bit of protectionism—mandated that only U.S. vessels and crews could operate within three miles of the U.S. coastline, thus barring help from anywhere else.

And of course, the teams cleaning up the BP spill had to contend with the Environmental Protection Agency, which might as well be renamed the Unintended Consequences Agency: Within days of the accident, the government of the Netherlands offered the world's most advanced skimming equipment to suck up the oil in the water—but the Environmental Protection Agency had a higher priority: the regulation that required that returned water be 99.985 percent pure, containing oil in a ratio of fifteen parts per million. It took more than a month before the paperwork on the skimmers showed that they, in fact, did so, a month during which the blown well was pouring more than sixty thousand barrels of oil into the Gulf every day.

Oh, and because skimming was—obviously—not the highest priority, oil reached shore, which resulted in another regulation, this one directly from the secretary of the interior, Ken Salazar, who decreed a moratorium on deepwater drilling. He was apparently indifferent to both the loss of twenty thousand well-paying jobs, the opposition of the National Academy of Engineering, and even a ruling by a U.S. District Court judge. The urge to regulate, it turns out, is *always* priority number one.

There's a reason, of course, that Progressives are so reflexively supportive of regulation, convinced that regulation is always their first solution, that a failure of regulation can always be solved by more regulation. Regulation is a way for smart people to tell everyone else what to do. And because regulations are government's way of substituting for the free market, they don't have to meet the first criterion of a market-based solution, which is that the costs shouldn't exceed the benefits. Regulators don't have to count, for example, the number of jobs lost because of their good intentions.

Entire books, of course, have been written about the job-killing consequences of regulation, even when—maybe especially when—the regulations are in conflict with another priority. The Obama administration has made some brave noises about support for more nuclear power plants but has done nothing to change the fact that China and France can build a nuclear power plant in three years, while in the United States it takes ten—entirely because of additional regulation and its inevitable partner: lots and lots of lawsuits.

But absolutely nothing illustrates the sheer idiocy of most regulation better than the American Recovery and Reinvestment Act (ARRA)—the $800 billion "stimulus bill" that was passed in February 2009—which has put so many regulatory strings on its money that it has practically written an encyclopedia of unintended consequences.

A simple example: $5 billion of the stimulus money was supposed to be used to pay for insulating homes. Without debating the underlying illogic of this—if insulating was worth doing, a private market would already exist for it at a lower cost—let's say it wasn't in the running to win the award as the dumbest project in the ARRA, a fierce competition that would range from the half million dollars budgeted for the Forest Service to replace the windows in a closed visitor center near Mount Saint Helens to the more than $300 million dollars allocated to a clean-energy program in partnership with (this is almost too easy) BP.

In Detroit, however, this money—which was, let's not forget, supposed to get money into the economy quick enough to *stimulate* it—took more than a year to find its way to the city agency responsible for weatherizing. Here's why:

- Advertisements for contractors failed to comply with regulations that required listing the precise wages being offered, which, to mollify unions, had to be the "prevailing wages" of the area as provided by the federal law.* It took *seven months*— from July 2009 to January 2010—to even figure out what the "prevailing wage" was.
- Because the insulating work had to comply with yet another set of regulations—the National Historic Preservation Act— documentation was needed for every house that was more than fifty years old: two to three weeks for each one, and Detroit

---

* For more on the law in question—the Davis-Bacon Act—see chapter 9.

has a *lot* of old homes (which are the ones that most benefit from insulation anyway).

As a result, this particular portion of stimulus ended up traveling so slowly that it was nearly a year before any of those dollars found their way into the hands of the American people.

It's not as if we don't have enough history to know that this sort of thing is pretty much inevitable. Back in the 1930s, similar policies were part of FDR's National Industrial Recovery Act, which offered antitrust exemptions to businesses if they raised wages. Companies in industries from auto production to chicken farming created (in order to get federal largesse) a code of "fair competition" designed to get rid of the "excessive competition" that the Roosevelt administration thought had caused the crisis. Well, the Act sure got rid of "excessive competition"—by cutting output, not exactly what a recovery needs. The result: It both distorted and delayed what might well have been a market-driven recovery from the Great Depression.

And though the NIRA was declared unconstitutional in 1935, many if not most of its policies survived. Some of them even survive to this day. The ARRA, for example, includes an almost identical "buy American" provision (originally drafted in 1933 to end the Depression—and *that* worked, didn't it?). The present-day version requires that all iron and steel used in ARRA projects be manufactured in the United States and, in addition to being completely useless, is so complicated that no one understands it. The cement used to make concrete on-site has to be American made, but not the concrete mixer or the shovels. The *exceptions* to this particular provision run for hundreds of pages, including a new and wonderful definition of "manufactured" (if it's assembled on-site, it's manufactured; if it was assembled elsewhere, it's—probably—not).

The ARRA was signed by the president on February 17, 2009. Bad as its regulations were, at least they were temporary: Once the stimulus had traveled through the economy, they would be gone. For the Restoring American Financial Stability Act of 2010, signed in July 2010 and better known as the Dodd-Frank Financial Reform Bill, regulation is forever.* And mysterious:

"Blake, tell me a rule you have at school."

"Well, we have to bring our homework or stay in the classroom during recess."

"Okay. What else?"

"We have to raise our hands before we talk. And we have to sit in our assigned seats. And—"

"That's enough. Let's call these the 'classroom rules.' What if one of the classroom rules was 'All fifth graders can't watch TV after eight o'clock?'"

"That's *not* a classroom rule!"

No, it isn't. On the other hand, people who love regulations can't help combining "home rules" with "classroom rules." The financial reform bill includes, among its 240 new regulations, a set of mine safety regulations (section 1503: Reporting Requirements Regarding Coal or Other Mine Safety), which you might think would be the responsibility of the Interior Department. It also includes a requirement that companies disclose any purchase of minerals from the Republic of the Congo (section 1502: Conflict Minerals). Like a teacher who tries to regulate behavior outside the classroom, legislators sometimes just can't stop themselves.

Regulators like regulating so much that they even compete with one another: Genetically modified crops have to wade through dozens if not hundreds of regulatory hearings held by the Department of Agriculture, the Environmental Protection Agency, *and* the Food and Drug Administration. And they don't always agree: Biotech

---

* For more on financial regulation, see chapter 2.

sugar beets approved by the Department of Agriculture, for example, can be banned under the National Environmental Policy Act; ones approved by the NEPA can be forbidden by the Department of Agriculture. The result, for fans of unintended consequences, is that the only companies able to survive this regulatory death of a thousand cuts are really big—which means that the regulations beloved of places like the Center for Food Safety, the Sierra Club, and the Organic Food Alliance (to recognize the plaintiffs in a lawsuit intended to ban biotech sugar beets) are actually forcing small companies out of the business altogether and leaving the field free for Monsanto and DuPont, neither of which is probably a favorite of the environmental lobby. Talk about unintended consequences.

And that's actually a big reason that free-market supporters find this so insidious. It isn't that they want unsafe food or dangerous mines or Congolese wars. It's that every new piece of legislation is a chance to pile new rules on the heads of American businesses, which are already drowning in the ones they have. In the end all I have to say is that brushing your teeth isn't a classroom rule.

Potentially the least offensive sort of regulation is the kind that requires manufacturers to tell customers just what's in their products. Though labeling regulations aren't cheap, a lot of their cost is actually what manufacturers call quality control: making sure that every batch of potato chips or shampoo or modeling clay contains the same ingredients as every other one. And while no business wants to share proprietary information with its competitors, anything that lowers the cost of comparing one product with another is generally beneficial to the economy; if businesses weren't required to share information about the amount of electricity your new washing machine used, it'd be harder—more expensive in time or money—to find the one you want. It wouldn't be impossible, of course: A trip to the library to read *Consumer Reports*, though, is a little more costly than just reading the label at Best Buy. If you must have regulations, those that reduce what economists call "information costs" are probably the least harmful. In fact, you can make a case that labeling regulations actually support free-market decision making because they leave the buying decision to the consumer: If I want to drive a gas guzzler, I can find the car with the worst mileage just as easily as the one with the best.

In practice, however, labeling regulations do a lot to reveal just what the urge to regulate is all about.

Here's how it always works. Progressive logic (if that's not a contradiction in terms) begins with the notion that everyone shares the same vision of the good life, that everyone, given a free choice, would decide to eat healthier food, use less fossil fuel, and (I guess) watch more public television and less Fox News. Since it's obvious that they don't always behave this way, it can only be because they have wrong, or not enough, information.

The answer is required labeling. Warning labels on cigarettes. Nutrition labels on food. Energy Star labels. Fuel economy labels. All of them giving information to consumers about the products they're buying.

However, since the impulse behind adding labels to millions upon millions of products wasn't to educate consumers but to change their behavior, the measure of the labels' effectiveness isn't how much information consumers have but what they do with it. And the goal of Progressives isn't to make sure that we know how much nicotine we are putting into our lungs, or saturated fat into our arteries, or gas guzzlers onto our roads, but to get us to stop doing so. Which means that so long as people are still buying cigarettes or Big Macs or muscle cars, the labels aren't doing the job. The next step, therefore, is to tweak the labels, which is why packs of cigarettes originally reminded us that smoking may be hazardous to our health and now rotate messages such as "Smoking by Pregnant Women May Result in Fetal Injury, Premature Birth, and Low Birth Weight" and "Cigarette Smoke Contains Carbon Monoxide." (In late 2010, the FDA proposed yet newer labels under the Cigarette Labeling and Advertising Act: images including a toe tag on a cadaver.)

And obviously, the increasing rates of obesity in America suggest that nutrition labels haven't done the job either. Think that they're already complicated enough, what with calories, calories from fat (and the amount of three different kinds of fat), carbohydrates, vitamins, and cholesterol? Marion Nestle, a nutrition professor at New York University (and one of the leaders of the "because it's good for you" movement), agrees. This is why she has turned her attention to the *front* of the package: the part people see on the shelf. And because the nutrition information that companies currently provide on package fronts is intended to help sell products (Oh no! Not *selling a product!*), it tends to focus on the stuff that people want in their foods, like fiber or whole grains. Professor Nestle and her colleagues at the Institute of Medicine are trying to get the Food and Drug Administration to require that food companies include the bad stuff—the amount of salt, calories, and fat—on the front of every package as well as on the nutrition label itself, because, as the professor says, "all of this is about food industry marketing. If it weren't about marketing, all this stuff would go off the packages and we would go back to packages that just said what the products were."

To Progressives, "marketing" is a dirty word.

It's not just the food police who get frustrated with the way people keep buying what they want, no matter how many times they're told it might not be good for them. The Environmental Protection Agency and the federal Department of Transportation have been labeling new cars with gas-mileage estimates ever since 1975, with the goal of persuading people to buy more fuel-efficient cars.* In August 2010, evidently out of concern that people were unable to figure out

---

* Yet another regulation—the Corporate Average Fuel Economy, or CAFE—tells automobile companies what the average mileage of cars has to be.

what "16MPG City/24MPG Highway" means, the EPA and DOT jointly announced a new labeling plan, under which cars would be given a letter grade depending on how virtuous—I mean economical—they were to drive. In order "to convince consumers to buy vehicles that use less energy," the new labels would give *A* grades to all-electric vehicles and plug-in hybrids—those that are "charged with an electric power cord and have small engines," while cars like the Ferrari 612 Scaglietti would get a *D* (apparently the EPA, like Progressive schools, can't bear to give an *F* to anyone). Which means that someone in Washington actually attended a meeting where everyone agreed that someone considering buying a $300,000 car with 530 horsepower is going to care whether it received a *D*—and that it mattered, given the two hundred or so Ferrari 612 Scagliettis sold in the United States annually.

Whether it's a law firm buying special chairs for its paralegals because of Occupational Safety and Health Administration "ergonomic" regulations or an independent trucker forced to send a 1099 tax form to every service station from which he buys more than $600 in gas annually,* regulations cost. A lot. At least one estimate is that the cost of federal regulations is more than 8 percent of America's GDP—and because a big chunk of that is hiring departments full of people to fill out forms, the costs fall most heavily on smaller businesses, which aren't big enough to have such people on staff.

There's a theory, in fact, that regulating is such an irresistible addiction for government that the number of regulations can't help but keep growing, under both Republican and Democratic administra-

---

* I'm not making up either of these. The Obama administration has reinstated the Clinton-era regulations intended to prevent carpal tunnel syndrome, regulations that will cost between $4 billion and $100 billion annually. And the new $600 gas threshold? Part of (don't laugh) health-care reform—a provision that even the *IRS itself* calls "disproportionate as compared with any resulting improvement in tax compliance" (IRS Report Number IR-2010-83, July 7, 2010, "National Taxpayer Advocate Submits Mid-Year Report to Congress").

tions. As government grows, so does regulation, and it's certainly true that some Republican administrations haven't exactly reduced the number of regulations that either stifle American growth or promote the interests of political cronies (usually both). Whatever you think about regulations, this theory goes, you can't really blame one party for the thousands of new ones coming out of Washington these days, since no matter who is in power, they keep adding regulations.

Nope.

As David Frum reminds me, when I was Blake's age, the federal government regulated the price of every ticket on every airline; the price of every cubic foot of natural gas; the size of the commissions that stockbrokers could charge; the amount of interest that could be paid on bank accounts; and even the content that radio and TV stations were required to broadcast in the form of political speech.

Some of these regulations, like the "fairness doctrine" that was the result of the Communications Act of 1934, date to the original New Deal. And some of the most costly regulations in American history are even older; it was the Roosevelt administration, after all, that presided over the end of the biggest regulatory fiasco in U.S. history: Prohibition.

But the president who really gave deregulation a good name—and so much else—was my hero: Ronald Reagan.* From the 1982 breakup of AT&T to the 1987 sale of Conrail (the publicly owned company formed to take over the assets of the Penn Central Railroad in 1976), President Reagan presided over the most significant deregulatory era in U.S. history—so significant that the portion of the American economy produced by highly regulated companies and industries, which represented more than 20 percent of the U.S. GDP

---

* We could give some credit to Jimmy Carter for deregulating the price of natural gas, but we'd have to take away points for the $20 billion he invested in the conversion of coal into natural gas because of a "shortage" that vanished once he deregulated its price. In fact, his deregulation-regulation-deregulation policies were so clumsy that—did I mention it was Jimmy Carter?

when he was inaugurated, had dropped to less than 7 percent by the time he left office in 1988. Less regulation meant more productivity— more people making and selling more stuff at lower prices. Does it surprise anyone that we still remember that era as one of America's most successful?

Which brings me back to Blake, and those laws preventing tickets from being sold at market prices. As you'll recall, Blake isn't very fussed about my paying market prices for tickets she wants, no matter what the regulations say. On the other hand . . .

"Dad?"

"Yes, Blake?"

"What's the price for our book?"

When she asked, the price on the book hadn't been set, but I tried to field the question.

"If what you're asking, Blake, is what people will pay for it, that depends."

"Depends on what?"

"Some stores sell books at full price, but a lot sell them at a discount."

"Discount?"

"Several dollars less."

"Less?! Why should someone pay less?!"

"Books aren't like tickets to a Reds game, Blake. If a game is real popular, the price of the seats goes up, because there's only one place to see the game and it has only so many seats. But if a book is popular, *lots* of places are selling it and competing for customers. So the best-selling books are the ones with the biggest discounts."

"So a lower price means we're selling more copies?"

"I think so."

"Well . . . that's okay."

We may make a capitalist out of Blake yet.

CHAPTER 8

August 2010: The $40 Ostrich Egg

August 2010: After avoiding the experience for years, Blake and I visited the country's most-written-about supermarket chain and survived to tell the tale.

You can't throw a rock in any parking lot in Short Hills, New Jersey, without hitting a car sporting an "Eat Local" bumper sticker. Whenever I see one, I'm tempted to throw the rock very hard, indeed.

The Kernen family, you see, doesn't make a point of buying locally grown food. Or organically raised chicken. Our only real encounter with the "slow food" movement is waiting for pizza delivery. We don't think this is any particular virtue. But neither is it a vice.

We do shop for food, of course. Our local supermarket is very happy to sell us turkey burgers, apples, grapes, butter, chocolate-chip ice cream, Froot Loops, about a hundred different kinds of bread, about a thousand different kinds of cheese (okay, maybe it just looks like a thousand), pet food, paper goods, cleaning products, over-the-counter medicines, and enough prepared foods to feed a regiment a different meal every day for six months. They'll even sell us wine and beer. When tourists from the less developed parts of the world visit the United States, the most reliable way to overwhelm them is not a trip to Yankee Stadium or the White House but by a simple visit to an ordinary American supermarket.

This is true when these supermarkets are compared not just with their equivalents in other parts of the world but with their equivalents in every other time in human history. And the sheer abundance is only the half of it; food has never been cheaper.

Take the loaf of bread for sale at our local grocery for $1.79 a pound. Two hundred years ago, that bread's cost, in labor, was more than two hours. Based on the current average U.S. hourly wage—a bit more than $22—the cost today is about five minutes. When I was Blake's age, the average U.S. family—such as, for example, mine—spent more than eleven cents out of every dollar of disposable income on groceries. Today that family spends only a bit more than five cents—a drop of more than 50 percent.

There are a lot of reasons for this, including higher wages, along with gigantic improvements in agricultural productivity and in the transportation available to move food from farm to table. One is the supermarket itself.

No one reading this book is old enough to remember when the dominant way Americans shopped for food was in over-the-counter markets, essentially unchanged from the general stores that Blake and Scott have only seen in western movies. In the 1920s, that started to change, primarily when the Great Atlantic & Pacific Tea Company—A&P, which at one time was responsible for taking in more than half the entire country's grocery-shopping dollars—started converting them to self-service groceries. In 1930, Michael "King" Cullen opened America's first recognizable supermarket in Jamaica, Queens, but it wasn't until after World War II that supermarkets really took off.

As they did, Americans started spending less and less on food. In 1930, when that first King Kullen opened, grocery shopping took twenty cents of the average American's disposable income. By 1947, when supermarkets were still a curiosity—depression and war had slowed their growth to a crawl—the number was down to nineteen cents. Ten years later, though, it had fallen to fifteen cents, twenty years later to nine cents, and, well, you know the rest.

By traditional measures, this is a triumph: more food for less labor than at any time in history. The much-debated costs of this particular triumph, obesity and related diseases, are, it seems to me, pretty high-class problems to have, at least in historical terms.

Not everyone agrees. There's at least one supermarket whose guiding philosophy is that Americans should pay *more* for their food.

Our local Whole Foods is pretty typical of the chain. Like most supermarkets, the produce is close to the entrance, though I think it's safe to say that some of the ingredients on offer are, well, unusual. One emu egg, for example, will set you back $29.95, which seems like a lot until you notice that an ostrich egg costs ten dollars more. The fact that it's supposed to make an omelet that will feed twelve to fourteen people (or a cake the size of a golf cart) might ease the sticker shock for some shoppers, but not me. Or Blake.

"Dad?"

"Yes, Blake?"

"Do people actually *eat* those?"

"I guess. Probably not very often."

Blake considered the ostrich egg again.

"You know what I think?"

"What, Blake?"

"I think they're showing off."

You bet. According to the folks at Whole Foods, an ostrich egg doesn't actually taste much different from chicken eggs, so it's a good bet that anyone who is paying six times what even Whole Foods charges for eggs from organically raised, free-range, and thoroughly contented chickens (and *fifteen* times what two dozen eggs cost at a normal supermarket) isn't doing it for the flavor. A big chunk of the appeal of Whole Foods, and places like it, is the fun of telling someone else about your superior taste.

Blake's favorite spot in the entire store, in fact, is the rack of weird and wonderful salts from around the world, including Alderwood Smoked Sea Salt and pink Himalayan rock salt, whose magical flavor that justifies a $15.99 per pound price (for salt!) we're not likely to find out about.

Though it's easy to make fun of Whole Foods' high-priced luxury foods, no free-market capitalist should be too fussed about them. After all, almost all luxury products, from Hartmann luggage to Armani ties, depend on some element of status appeal, and while we do our best to teach Blake and Scott that it's usually a bad idea to spend a lot for a label, free-market means freedom to spend your money any way you want. John Mackey, the supermarket chain's founder, is probably as well known for his libertarian economic beliefs as for his free-range eggs.

There are, however, some less harmless aspects to the Whole Foods experience, which has evolved a lot from its health-food-store origins. The "health food" audience was—and remains—convinced that food that includes ingredients like the preservatives and stabilizers that make it possible to ship food all over the world without spoiling were, on the scale of healthiness, somewhere between drinking weed killer and chewing razor blades. In fact, simply eliminating the taint of artificial preservatives and flavorings—and especially artificial sweeteners (obesity is the one health issue that Whole Foods completely ignores)—isn't enough. A typical Whole Foods devotes at least three aisles to nutritional supplements, vitamins, homeopathic medicines, antioxidants, eleuthero (I don't know what this is, either), and black cohosh (ditto). And as if that weren't enough, literally dozens of different foods, from yogurt to breakfast cereal, are now forti-fied with strains of something called "probiotic" bacteria.

You might think that Whole Foods shoppers—and anyone spending serious money on nutritional supplements—would have a problem explaining why, by any measure, the human life span and quality of life have continued to improve at almost the same rate that the food industry has added deadly poisons to the diet. Think again. A true devotee doesn't care about the lack of any proof that organic food is healthier and sneers at the sort of study done by the *American Journal of Clinical Nutrition*, which reviewed more than 160 papers published over the last fifty years and found that organic food offers no nutritional advantage over conventionally grown food. Despite the safest food supply in human history (the fact that outbreaks of *E. coli*—whose incidence of contamination in beef has *fallen* 45 per-cent since 2000—and salmonella are now front-page news is actually a testament to their rarity; *all* food-borne illnesses are responsible for only a third as many annual deaths as, say, alcohol-based liver dis-ease), the nutrition-paranoia business is healthier than ever. After all, even if people aren't keeling over from unclean food and water, they're still getting cancer—and cancer takes long enough to appear, and is mysterious enough in its origins, that preventing it is the number one reason people try to improve their health nutritionally.

Now, I don't claim to know a whole lot about nutrition. But I spent a good bit of my youthful academic life working at the most prestigious cancer labs in the world, under the supervision of Nobel Prize winners (one of the reasons I now earn my living commenting on the world of finance is the realization that I might be smart—but not *that* smart), and I can say, with a great deal of confidence, that cancers are so diverse and their causes so varied and complex that the whole notion that organic food is less likely to cause a malignancy is just about as sensible as throwing salt over your shoulder or practicing animal sacrifice.

That salt would be, of course, Alderwood Smoked Sea Salt. And the animals for the sacrifice: only free range and grass fed.

It's probably a little unfair to hammer Whole Foods for what is a much more widespread set of delusions. The fetish of the moment is for food that is "organic, local, and slow"—food that is grown or raised without anything artificial, as (mostly) protection against cancer; grown or raised within fifty miles (or so) from the kitchen table where it is eaten, to protect the planet against climate change from the burning of fossil fuels; and grown, raised, and especially prepared in the slowest, least industrialized way possible, to restore a lost golden age when Ma made pies from scratch and Pa picked the corn fresh for dinner. It's practically an article of faith to Progressives and, sad to say, to a lot of other folks who should know better.

And as I mentioned above, we Kernens don't really have a huge problem with people deciding to spend their money on organic food or pink Himalayan sea salt; free markets are free. If Michael Pollan, professor of journalism at UC Berkeley and author of local-organic-and-slow classics like *The Omnivore's Dilemma*, wants to eat paté made from a wild boar he killed, gutted, and dressed in the Berkeley hills, then good for him. At the very least he's probably helping to defend Berkeley from wild boar attacks. The problem with Pollan and other gurus of the movement, like Alice Waters of Chez Panisse restaurant in—wait for it—Berkeley or Michelle Obama and her White House kitchen garden, is that they aren't satisfied just to wallow in their own virtue—to argue, as Pollan did in an interview with the *Wall Street Journal*, that eggs *should* cost $8 a dozen. Like most Progressives, they are determined to make everyone else just as virtuous as they are. This is always done for our own good, which is the same thing I said when we had our dog neutered.

Even this kind of self-righteousness would be easier to take if it weren't expressed with such confident ignorance. Attacking modern farmers for applying "industrial" science to their soil, for testing it chemically for nutrients and acidity, for correcting levels of nitrogen and phosphorus, and especially for the specialization that permits fewer than 2 percent of the U.S. population to feed the other 98 percent (this is one-tenth the number of only sixty years ago) is a bit like demanding that we go back to copying books by hand, which would at least cut down on the number of Michael Pollan books. Eliminate herbicides? If so, better be prepared to eliminate no-till farming, which decreases soil erosion by millions of tons a year. Say no to factory-made nitrogen fertilizers? Okay, but Norman Borlaug,* the Nobel laureate, agronomist, and father of the Green Revolution, which freed nations like India and Mexico from famine, estimated that the planet can support only four billion people using purely natural sources. If Europe tried to feed itself organically, it would need to put under cultivation an amount of land equal to the remaining forests of France, Germany, Britain, and Denmark combined.

Even on environmental grounds, organic food is a solution in search of a problem—one that industrial food production is already solving. Food production in the industrial world increased 5 percent between 1990 and 2004—on 4 percent *less* land, producing 4 percent *less* greenhouse gas emissions, and using 17 percent *less* synthetic nitrogen. The reasons are largely an infusion of technology: drip irrigation on fields leveled with lasers to reduce runoff and GPS-equipped tractors that automatically keep equipment on straighter paths and plot location down to the meter, allowing them to use chemicals only where needed. Infrared sensors are now used to identify the color of crops, calculating where fertilizer is needed and where it isn't. It's not the sort of technology that was used back in the days when the average farm was less than one hundred acres. And farms weren't that small

---

* Borlaug, who died in 2009, also estimated that it would take an additional five billion cows to produce enough "natural" fertilizer to produce the needed nitrogen, to say nothing of uncounted tons of methane, a greenhouse gas. How Progressives can, at the same time, be against both global warming and synthetic fertilizers (and Borlaug himself, who supported intensive agriculture as the best defense against deforestation) escapes me. But they are. At a 2002 meeting in Rome that included Friends of the Earth and Greenpeace, the final conference report blamed the Green Revolution for the rise in world hunger.

because of farmers' desire to live closer to the land; that was the amount of land that could be cultivated by animal power alone.

Of course, a significant number of Whole Foods shoppers are sort of down on animal power, as well. In fact, they're sort of down on animal *anything*. They're called vegans.

Vegans are, of course, what happens when vegetarians feel a need for even *more* self-righteousness and make a point of avoiding not only meat but also milk, eggs, and any other product derived from what they call the "subjugation" of animals, like gelatin, leather, or wool. How they resolve this with the thousands of insects they "subjugate" in the course of driving their electric cars (or riding their bicycles) or the billions of bacteria they destroy every time they brush their teeth is a complete mystery.

And anyway, the nonvegan organic-food activists probably want to return to animal power as well, since the internal-combustion engines at the heart of both farm machinery and the trucks that deliver farm produce to market are, to the same Progressive mind-set, modern farming's most dangerous aspect of all.

Unlike most ten-year-olds, Blake has already developed a taste for coffee, which is not so wonderful, since her energy level is already at the point where the caffeine in a single Coca-Cola works a lot like turbocharging a Corvette. On the other hand, I wish I got a similar jolt from my morning cup of coffee—no surprise when you remember my work day starts well before 5 A.M.

The coffee I drink every morning isn't anything special. I neither need nor want the various specialty coffees that have made Starbucks into a billion-dollar brand (and certainly don't need the calories in their lattes or Frappuccinos). Even so, I am impressed with the sheer range of coffees for sale in even a normal supermarket. There's French roast. Special morning blend. Hawaiian Kona. Jamaican Blue Mountain. Ethiopian harrar. Low acid. Espresso ground. Fair trade.

Fair trade?

....

"Dad?"

"Yes, Blake?"

"Is this spelled right? Is it the same as 'free trade'?"

Not much.

The first time I saw the term, I was as confused as Blake and had to do a little digging to find out just what the noble-sounding term "fair trade" actually meant. As usual with the sort of feel-good economics so beloved of Progressives, there's a lot less here than meets the eye. Fair trade, in one form or another, has been around for nearly fifty years, but until the late 1980s it was mostly a way for Western liberals to assuage their guilt about their own prosperity by paying a higher price for handicrafts like jute shopping bags, straw hats, and rope sandals in the belief that some of their money would find its way back to the rural villages where the stuff was made. For the last twenty years or so, "fair trade" labeling organizations—there are at least four—have certified that the chain of transactions that leads back to commodities like cocoa, sugar, and especially coffee wasn't enriching "middlemen" at the expense of farmers.

Middlemen are a favorite villain of Progressives, because—in Progressive World—they don't add anything of value to a transaction. Never mind that without trucks, warehouses, shipping companies, more warehouses, more trucks, packaging companies, *more* warehouses, *more* trucks, and, of course, supermarkets—or even farmers' markets—it's pretty hard to get coffee or anything else into even a Progressive pantry.

The people pushing Fair Trade—by now it's always capitalized and sometimes made into a single word, "Fairtrade"—say they support free trade but spend a lot more time on its failures than on its successes. Even so, labeling coffee Fair Trade and charging an additional four or five bucks a pound for the stuff shouldn't be a huge problem for a free-market guy like me. If people want to pay a premium, why not?

There, are, it turns out, several reasons for a free-market purist to object to the fair-trade concept—and only one of them is that it sounds so patronizing.

"Blake, what would you call something that wasn't a fair trade?"
"An unfair one?"

Exactly. But the sneering attempt of fair-trade coffee (or fair-trade anything) to stigmatize any other sort is the least of its problems. More important is that it replaces the enormous power of the market to allocate resources efficiently with a bunch of good intentions—and everyone knows where they lead. Fair trade, by setting a floor price on coffee beans, certainly offers an incentive to farmers to grow them. But the difference between the fair-trade price and the market price is nothing more than charity; and worse, it is charity offered only to farmers who agree to continue producing the same stuff, in the same way, that made them poor—and eligible for charity—in the first place. This isn't just theory. Every one of the fair-trade licensing organizations discourages diversification and mechanization, pesticides, fertilizers—you name it. Coffee farms, to qualify as fair-trade suppliers, have to be smaller than twelve acres, and they're not permitted to employ any full-time staff.

And even as charity, it's not exactly a success story. Only about 5 percent—*5 percent*—of the fair-trade price actually makes it back to the producers anyway. Partly this is because the raw commodity is only part of the final product. And partly it's because of the cost of fair trade itself. An executive at the biggest fair-trade coffee cooperative in Guatemala is on record saying that "after paying for the cooperative's employees and programs, nothing remained of the Fairtrade premiums to be passed on to the individual farmers."

Worst of all, fair trade discourages *any* sort of innovation, even the sort that results in the kind of expensive coffee that is (to really devoted coffee drinkers) actually worth a higher price. Fair trade sets a minimum of $1.26 a pound for green (i.e., unroasted) coffee beans, which is a lot more than the market price for ordinary coffee but a lot less than the $1.60 or more paid for high-quality beans. What this means is that consumers who have bought into the fair-trade propaganda are not only buying inferior coffee but are also refusing to buy coffee that puts even more of their money into the hands of coffee producers. The answer isn't reducing their exposure to free markets: As William Easterly of NYU's Development Research Institute— not exactly a hotbed of conservative thought—writes, "the parts of the world that are still poor are suffering from too little capitalism."

It's not very hard to figure out why Colombia is a better place to grow coffee than, say, Kansas. Though seventy different countries are home to coffee farms and plantations, all of them are located in a pretty narrow geographic band, from about twenty-three degrees north to maybe twenty-five degrees south—Havana to São Paulo— which is the only place the coffee berries can grow. Since most of the world's coffee drinkers are located outside the coffee belt, the countries within it enjoy a commercial advantage that explains why millions of their farmers are able make their livings growing and, less frequently, roasting and exporting coffee beans.

This kind of advantage is what economists call an *absolute advantage*, and it applies to all sorts of things that are found not just in supermarkets but also in your average ten-year-old's closet.

"Blake?"

"Yes, Daddy?"

"Go up to your bedroom and pick out ten of your shirts, then bring them down here."

. . . .

Here's the list of countries in which Blake's assortment of T-shirts, button-downs, and turtlenecks were manufactured: China, Vietnam, Indonesia, Pakistan, China (again), India, Bangladesh, Costa Rica, India (again), and Mexico.

"Why do think so many of your shirts were made in these countries?"

"Because they're good at making them?"

They sure are. The United States imports more than $100 billion worth of clothes every year, and despite our clothing bills, only a small fraction of it ends up in one Kernen closet or another. The reason that so much of it comes from developing countries is, as Blake guessed, that they're good at it. Their absolute advantage isn't, however, that Honduran or Chinese or Bangladeshi clothing factories are better or more up to date than those in the United States but that they are a *lot* cheaper to run. The wages paid to workers in those countries are so much lower that it is almost impossible for Americans to compete (which is a subject for another book). It's no great trick to show Blake that the reason her tie-dyed V-neck only cost $4.99 to buy is that it's just plain cheaper to make it in Vietnam than in North Carolina—though it can confuse the average member of Congress.

However, a whole lot of other things we import from other countries can be made even more inexpensively here, which *really* confuses a lot of members of Congress. The reason we buy so many gazillion gallons of imported soft drinks is not that Mexican bottling plants are more efficient than those in the United States; in fact, those bottling plants south of the Rio Grande are making the same Pepsi-Cola, using the same sort of factories, as those in the United States. The reason is the counterintuitive concept known as *comparative advantage.*

The idea of comparative advantage is centuries old, dating back to (at least) 1817, when an economist named David Ricardo* used it to explain why, even though both wine and cloth were cheaper to make in Portugal than in Britain, Britain imported only wine from Portugal. Cloth, you see, was only a little cheaper to make in Portugal, while wine was much cheaper. It made sense for the Portuguese to specialize in the area where they had the biggest edge—the largest comparative advantage—and make wine, while buying cloth from British factories.

Inspired by reading about Ricardo, I decided to explain to Blake why the United States imports so much stuff from overseas that we are perfectly capable of making at home. Out came the pencils and paper, while Blake managed to choke down her groans.

"Have you ever heard the expression 'You can't compare apples and oranges'?"

"Yup."

"Well, we're going to do just that. Let's imagine two different farms—"

"Where are they?"

"Doesn't matter."

"I mean, are they in different states, or different countries?"

"Okay. Let's say that they're in different countries. One is in the USA, and the other's in—"

"South Africa."

(I should point out that the World Cup was going on while this particular exercise was under way.)

"Okay. South Africa. Now let's say that the United States farm can harvest four hundred apples a month and two hundred oranges,

---

* Ricardo was, like me, a onetime stockbroker, but—unlike me—he got *really* rich doing it. When he retired from the stock exchange to write books such as *The Principles of Political Economy*, he was worth somewhere north of half a million pounds—somewhere between $500 million and $1 billion in today's dollars.

while the South African farm can harvest two hundred apples and fifty oranges."

"Okay."

"Let's make a chart."

	APPLES	ORANGES
American farm	400	200
South African farm	200	50
Total	600	250

"Now, which can grow the most oranges in a month?"

"The U.S., of course."

"But the U.S. can also make the most apples, right?

"Right."

"So what's the most apples *and* oranges we can get out of these two farms?"

"Well, six hundred apples and two hundred fifty oranges?"

"Okay. Now how about this: The farmers can decide to plant more of one kind of tree than another, but if the South African farmer decides to shift from apples to oranges, he's going to lose four apples for every orange he grows. On the other hand, the American farmer only loses two apples for every orange *he* grows. Advantage U.S., right?"

"He could grow more oranges."

"But the South African farmer has the same advantage in apples. If he stops growing oranges completely, he's going to get four apples for each orange he gives up. So by giving up his fifty oranges, he gets . . . ?"

"Two hundred more apples. Four hundred in all."

"And now the American farmer can grow all the oranges he wants."

Time for a new chart:

	Apples	Oranges
American farm	240	280
South African farm	400	0
Total	640	280

The result is forty more apples *and* thirty more oranges, all for the same amount of work on the same amount of land. American oranges can be traded for South African apples, and everyone is better off, *even though the most efficient apple farm isn't growing the most apples.*

This is why free trade is so important and why the idea of local sufficiency in food is such a dangerous idea. And when I say "dangerous," I don't mean just to everyone's wallet.

Around the world, 850 million people are undernourished. Not obese, undernourished. A lot of Progressives—the sort that are reflexively against any sort of technological or commercial progress—argue that this is because of a lot of unjust exploitation by big agricultural businesses who have bid up the price for food. They are (surprise!) wrong. Almost all of the people in the world who are just one harvest away from famine couldn't care less about the world market price for corn or rice or soybeans. All of them, by definition, have *some* comparative advantage, but without any ability to trade whatever is produced by that advantage, they are doomed to chronic poverty and malnutrition.

But at least they're organic (poor farmers can't afford either fertilizer or pesticides, so their food is as organic as anything Michael Pollan eats), local (more than 70 percent of African rural households live more than a thirty-minute walk from the nearest all-weather road), and very, very slow.

CHAPTER 9

September 2010: Look for the Union Label: You're Paying for It

In September 2010, the Kernens go out on the town—and start thinking about labor unions.

Though we live less than an hour away from America's theater capital, Penelope and I don't get to see many Broadway shows, mostly because of the early-to-bed-early-to-rise demands of *Squawk Box*'s schedule. However, after the tenth time my friend Barry Habib insisted that the Kernens needed to spend an evening at the theater, I couldn't say no. The evening in question was a Saturday-night performance of *Rock of Ages*, a "jukebox musical" with songs from 1980s bands like Journey, Twisted Sister, and Bon Jovi—and Barry knew something about the show because he was the musical's lead producer.

And we had a great time. There's a reason that the show was nominated for five Tony Awards, after all. And why it's been that rarest of things: a hit Broadway musical.

You'd think, in fact, that with full houses, a national touring company, and plans for a movie, all would be sunny in Barry's world. Mostly, you'd be right; he's an optimistic guy. But he does notice some pretty dark clouds on the horizon.

"It's simple," Barry says. "We're working for our own unions instead of our audiences."

It's not a problem getting Barry talking about the unions that dominate every aspect of a Broadway production, from the electricians who operate every light switch to the actors themselves. And his talk isn't exactly positive.

This isn't because Barry is reflexively antiunion: He's even a member of the Screen Actors Guild himself. But his real instincts are those of an entrepreneur, which isn't surprising, because he's been starting up businesses—successful businesses—since he was in his twenties, in everything from manufacturing and selling electronics to packaging mortgages. Like most successful businessmen, Barry is all about growing the business—or as he put it to me, "Okay, we have a success. How can it be *more* successful? How can we generate more ticket sales?"

The question was a rhetorical one, but he had a pretty good answer: Since the most loyal and motivated buyers of his product—tickets to *Rock of Ages*—were the people who had already seen the show at least once, Barry figured that he could capitalize on that—and the best time to capture the attention of those buyers was when they were already at the show and having the same kind of fun that Penelope and I had when we saw it.

So, Barry thought, let's make them an offer: Anyone who agreed to purchase tickets for a subsequent performance of the show on the same day they had just seen it could do so at a discount. So far, so good, but doing it at the ticket office would require—because of the standard union agreement—paying overtime to the ticket-sales staff. Instead, Barry wanted to make the offer during intermission; and since the show features a digital screen behind the stage, why not advertise the deal there?

Why not? Because putting *anything* on that digital screen—a single word, even—required the attention of a union member and cost $600.

Or try this one: The Brooks Atkinson Theatre, where *Rock of Ages* was packing them in—it's since moved three blocks away, to the Helen Hayes Theatre—is, like a lot of Broadway theaters, old. The walls and pillars that have been holding up the roof since it was built in 1926 aren't as well situated as you might like, and as a result, a few dozen of the house's thousand-plus seats—those on the extreme right and left—have obstructed views of part of the stage.

On Broadway, you can't let anything go to waste, so those seats were for sale, but at half price. Barry, who was understandably eager to maximize the show's profitability, had an idea: Install two fifty-inch flat-screen monitors on either side of the stage and have two high-definition cameras send a closed-circuit signal to fill in those portions of the stage invisible to those seated in the obstructed seats. They get a better experience; the show gets to sell the tickets at full price. Everyone wins.

Except . . .

Here's how Barry explained it to me.

"How much do you think it would cost to buy two top-end fifty-inch monitors and high-def cameras?"

"I don't know . . . ten thousand dollars?"

"And to install them?"

"Another five thousand?"

The cost to add the monitors and cameras was, in fact, $120,000. The reason is that twenty-six different dues-paying union members were required.

The real cost, though, of these union work rules isn't just the money. It's that a smart businessman like Barry Habib isn't very likely to invest in another show, despite the success of *Rock of Ages*. Like anyone in business, Barry likes to think that talent and hard work are the keys to succeeding, but in his judgment, Broadway's unions have made the theater into a crap game—one with loaded dice.

I tried to explain this to Blake.

. . . .

"Blake, do you remember when we had our new television installed?"

"Sure."

"How many people did the job?"

"Two, I think."

"What if I told you that installing a TV just like this one in a New York theater needs twenty-six people?"

"Is New York better?

"No, Blake. The folks in New Jersey are just as good at their jobs as the ones in New York. But working in New York is like hiring a really good plumber not just to fix the faucet but also to turn it on whenever you want a drink."

"No one would do that. It's stupid."

Well, yes. But most stupid things started out sounding pretty sensible; once upon a time, that electrical job at the Brooks Atkinson Theatre wasn't something you could buy off the shelf at Best Buy. And there are still a lot of skills needed from a plumber, or an electrician, or a carpenter, and their respective unions make a lot of noise advertising that the only way you can guarantee those skills is by hiring someone with a union card. Whether this is true or not—you can get an earful from both sides of the debate—this argument is what makes them just the latest version of the original "unions" of artisans: guilds.

Trying to answer Blake's questions forced me to do a little digging into the history of guilds and unions. And what I've learned is that though organizations like guilds have been around (probably) as long as people have been specializing in skills, it was during the Middle Ages that they really got going and established the triangular organization that survives to this day among artisans like carpenters and electricians: apprentice, journeyman (who tended to "journey" from workshop to workshop), and master.

The Industrial Revolution was a funeral for traditional guilds.

The father of the free market, Adam Smith, hated them, largely because of their habit of adding costs to the economy,* but those costs were probably affordable where the value of consistent performance outweighed the costs of the guild labor. So long as you could count on a guild-woven tapestry or guild-built cabinet to be superior to one from an unknown artisan, you were willing to pay a premium to a member of the guild, both for his skill and for his access to the techniques kept secret by the guild. With industrialization, the cost of keeping such techniques private started to look like a pretty bad bargain. The Netherlands abolished guilds in 1784. France followed suit in 1791—though French guilds transformed themselves into "mutual aid societies" after 1815 and survive to this day, paralyzing the entire country every few months with national strikes. The same transformation happened in the United States, which had the same apprentice-journeyman-master guilds as Britain until the middle of the nineteenth century, when they turned into craft unions, essentially guilds without the secret passwords and initiations.

The value of craft unions to their members is obvious: higher pay. Their value to the people who buy their services is the seal of approval that a union card gives to its holder. And given the costs of fixing mistakes made by a plumber or an electrician who doesn't know what's what, I'm usually happy to pay extra for that union card myself. It's the same reason that I kind of like the idea that Blake and Scott's pediatrician has "MD" after her name. It's libertarian gospel to criticize all unions, but true craft unions are, at worst, a pretty small problem.

Most union members, however, aren't members of craft unions,

---

* One historian I found—Richard Sennett, in his book *The Craftsman*—described guilds as protecting the artisan "not only from external competition, but also from the competition of his fellow-members [thus leading to] the destruction of all initiative. No one was permitted to harm others by methods which enabled him to produce more quickly and more cheaply than they. Technical progress took on the appearance of disloyalty."

the ones that organize members "horizontally"—all of the welders at fifty different machine shops, for example.

Even Barry Habib's electricians, though they are unquestionably skilled technicians, are members of an "industrial" union: the International Alliance of Theatrical Stage Employees, Moving Picture Technicians, Artists and Allied Crafts of the United States, Its Territories and Canada, or IATSE. It's with industrial unions, organizing the workforces of entire companies and even industries, that unions start to have some real impact on free markets. And the impact isn't positive.

There used to be some real conflict—baseball-bat-and-brass-knuckles kind of conflict—between craft and industrial unions. The umbrella organization for America's craft unions, the original American Federation of Labor, insisted that the key thing laborers had in common was *what* they did; its competitor, the Congress of Industrial Organizations, thought that what mattered was *where* they worked. As huge factories replaced small workshops, this made industrial unions, like the United Auto Workers, a lot more successful, because they were willing to represent the unskilled workers who made up an ever larger part of the workforce in those factories.

With this, the economic value of unions to the buyers of their services—the guarantee of *some* level of training and skill—pretty much vanished. But in return, the economic value to the members themselves grew dramatically. The leverage of a few hundred carpenters or shoemakers was insignificant compared to that of a hundred thousand miners or auto workers, and each member benefited accordingly.

It's no accident that the ascent of industrial unionism, like Keynesianism, the New Deal, and other triumphs of the Progressive agenda, occurred during the Great Depression. Union membership, which would grow until it covered nearly a third of the entire U.S. workforce by the 1950s, was yet another expression of the idea that no matter what the Constitution said about the matter, people weren't free at all. They were actually subject to such large forces outside their own control that they couldn't take care of themselves, which meant that someone else needed to take care of them. Given the economic hardships of the day, it's hard not to be sympathetic to the desire of *any* worker to do whatever looked like it might improve the chances of not just keeping a job but also ensuring that employers paid the highest possible wages. It makes emotional (if not economic) sense to fight back against the large employers who were the apparent reason that jobs were so hard to come by in the first place.

However, the unions didn't stop there. Unions represented not just millions of *laborers* but also millions of *voters*.

Politics isn't exactly a business; politicians don't really have to worry about the costs and benefits of their decisions in the same way a factory owner does. However, their actions are still economically rational: They produce laws, which they use to buy votes. If what they sell of the former is valuable enough to buy enough of the latter, they get reelected—and this is true even without bringing corruption into the picture. Which is why, starting in the 1930s with the rise of industrial unionism, legislators started passing a *lot* of new laws designed to appeal to millions of existing and potential union members.

I confess that I didn't know a lot of this when I started this project. But what I learned was eye-opening.

"Blake?"

"Yes, Dad?"

"You know the pet store where you buy your fish supplies?"

"Sure."

"And the people who work there?"

"Yeah?"

"Now let's say that you wanted a job there when you were older. And you were competing for a job with someone who had a lot more experience—"

"COULD I?!"

"Not so fast: What if the only way it was worth hiring you was that you were willing to work for less money—"

"I WOULD!"

"—but you couldn't, because there was a rule that said that everyone who worked in a pet store in New Jersey had to be paid the same as everyone else."

"NOT FAIR!"

Nope. But that's pretty much the case with the Davis-Bacon Act of 1931, which required employers to pay "prevailing wages" on federal projects. Since "prevailing wage" was just a code word for union scale, this ensured that employers couldn't save money by hiring nonunion labor on government construction work, even when nonunion laborers were willing to work for less. The original champions of the Davis-Bacon Act made no bones about this, nor about its racist origins; William Green, the president of the AFL, even went on record saying, "Colored labor is being brought in to demoralize wage rates."[*]

Davis-Bacon was just the start. Once unions realized that they weren't just collective-bargaining agents for their members but also political players with votes—and money—to offer, they began systematically agitating for laws that benefited members. And they didn't care who paid for those benefits, which was almost the economy at large: employers, and especially nonunion labor. The Norris-LaGuardia Act of 1932, for example, prevents courts from issuing injunctions against strikes even if they violate a no-strike provision in an earlier contract. But the big one came along three years later in the form of the National Labor Relations Act of 1935.

---

[*] Just in case you think this is an artifact of the past, Davis-Bacon is still in place eighty years later: It was an explicit part of the Obama administration's American Recovery and Reinvestment Act of 2009 (the stimulus bill), even for projects funded only "in part" by the federal government.

The NLRA was sold to the public as a way to prohibit any sort of coercion of employees by management. It still is. What a lot of people don't know—I didn't—is that it also *authorizes* exactly the same sort of coercion by employees against their coworkers: NLRA is majority rule on steroids.

"Blake?"

"Yes, Dad?"

"How many kids are in your class?"

"Nineteen."

"Okay. What if ten of you voted to spend half an hour on a piece of homework, and nine of you wanted to spend as much time as you wanted?"

"I'd vote to take as much time as I wanted."

"And what if everybody had do whatever the majority decided?"

Blake's eye rolling was pretty much all the answer I needed. But what makes no sense to her is the essence of the NLRA, which obliges employers to negotiate with only one union representing its employees and to enforce any agreement, even against employees who hadn't even voted to join the union in the first place. In fact, in its original form, the NLRA could require membership in the union— and even today, unions can collect dues from nonmembers if they are covered by a union contract. If you think it's okay to be required *by law* to give your dollars to someone who is going to use them to (for example) support political candidates that you may despise, you probably don't have a problem with this. But you should keep in mind what it means, which is that if you're a working in a unionized workplace, federal law states that you no longer "own" your own labor; a majority of your coworkers does.

It's not so hard to get grumpy about the coercion inherent in unionization; no one likes being forced to do something they wouldn't choose on their own, and forcing at least *some* workers to finance union activities is pretty much unavoidable, once you let unions in the door at all. But it's also not so hard to understand why unions get started in the first place: Everyone wants more money, and the one thing that unions unquestionably do is raise wages for their members over what the market would otherwise pay. (But it's not certain that unions actually deliver a long-term advantage to their members: If manufacturers pass the cost of higher wages along to their customers, then the advantage is temporary, because of price inflation.)

But a book about free-market economics should probably figure out whether unionization is, on balance, good or bad (or possibly just neutral) for the economy as a whole. After all, even if Ford Motor Company is "hurt" by paying an average of $75 an hour in salary and benefits to its UAW members, that doesn't necessarily mean that the U.S. economy is worse off, any more than the New York City economy is worse off because the Yankees pay Derek Jeter—a member in good standing of the Major League Baseball Players Association— $17 million a year.

What *does* make the impact on the economy negative is when unions are successful in raising wages above what workers could command if they were in a competitive marketplace. And while this is pretty obvious today—unions raise the wages of members up to 30 percent over those of comparable nonunion workers[*]—it was actually a pretty big "if" for a lot of workers during the first decades of trade unionism. Wherever employers operated as "monopsonies" (if a product or service has only one seller, it's a monopoly; if it has only one *buyer*, it's a monopsony), the labor marketplace was the opposite of competitive, and you can make a decent case that unions counteracted one negative force with another. Since monopsonies were rampant in early industrial America—there were entire towns where the

---

[*] Probably as a direct corollary, unionized industries produce 2 percent to 3 percent *less* job growth annually than nonunionized ones.

only employer was a single coal mine or steel plant—it's not too surprising that unions found such places fertile ground for organizing workers.

Even during the heyday of trade unionism—basically from the 1930s to the 1950s—unions were appealing to the fraternal impulses of potential members as much as to their wallets. Unions were places of "brotherhood" and "solidarity." The union hall for the shoemakers of my hometown, Cincinnati (which had been a pretty congenial place for craft unions since the Civil War), was built like a church—a church with a lot of pool tables—and described as a "labor temple" by "Brother" William Prout.

But like a whole lot of things about unions, brotherhood and solidarity are things that sound good but have some significant hidden costs. The biggest of these is the tendency to argue that the value of every worker is the same as that of every other worker; brothers shouldn't compete with one another, whether they are members of the same family or of the same union. The only exception (as with families) is the privilege of being an older brother—or, in union terms, having more seniority in a job.

This isn't exactly a recipe for increasing productivity. The fundamental problem with unions is that they reward the very human desire to lock in advantage once achieved. This is why they are inevitably hostile to the dynamism that is at the heart of free-market capitalism. Union apologists, in the Obama administration and elsewhere, can argue that while unions raise wages, they also promote productivity because of union training and reduced turnover. However, any such value is (a) so modest that you have to squint to find it in the economic literature; and (b) *always* less than the union-wage increases that accompany labor negotiations. What this means is that even when productivity in a unionized company is growing, wages grow even faster. And when wages increase faster than productivity, jobs decrease, as manufacturers have incentives to replace workers with machinery.

If replacing dues-paying United Auto Workers members with robots to assemble cars were the biggest impact of union intransigence about wages, it wouldn't be so bad: Productivity increases are *always* good for the economy. But the perversities of unions, and especially their ability to write laws regulating labor, frequently result in much worse outcomes. Consider the case of United Parcel Service.

UPS, like most businesses of comparable size, is subject to the National Labor Relations Act and is therefore a union shop. Specifically, it has a labor contract with the International Brotherhood of Teamsters, one of the country's largest unions.* However, from the time it was founded, Federal Express, the primary competitor of UPS, was regulated not by the NLRA but by the Railway Labor Act of 1926 (it's a long story having to do with the fact that railroads and railroad employees were already subject to a different law that separated them as a labor class in the 1930s—yet another example of the ways unions—and government—distort the free market). Which is why, as Nick Gillespie reported in *Reason* magazine in 2009, UPS—and its Teamster "partners"—got Congress to include language in a bill reclassifying FedEx so that all of its nonpilot employees would be subject to the NLRA as well, thus giving the Teamsters carte blanche to organize—and raise FedEx's costs. The costs—to FedEx shareholders and customers—are likely to be measured in the tens, if not hundreds, of millions of dollars.

On April 24, 2010, the Public Employee of the Year Awards were broadcast to a national television audience for the first time. Among the candidates for the coveted title was Dennis Cosgrove, a school custodian from the borough of Queens, in New York City. His quali-

---

* And the one with the longest and best-known connection with organized crime in America. It would be easy to classify unions as "good" or "bad" based on their association with criminals, but I'm not sure that the economic cost of "good" unions is any less than that of "bad" ones.

fications included the 3,200 hours he managed to work in the preceding year—all of it overtime. Cosgrove's accomplishment is even more remarkable when you consider that he lives in Florida full time.

Dennis Cosgrove is, I am happy to report, a fictional character. His moment of televised glory came courtesy of the writers of *Saturday Night Live*. Nothing like this could actually happen.

Then again . . .

In September 2008, the *New York Times* reported on the curious fact that thousands of retirees from the publicly owned Long Island Rail Road had somehow managed to "earn" more than $200 million in disability payments over the preceding eight years. In fact, nearly 97 percent of *everyone* who retired during that period applied for and received average disability payments of about $3,000 a month. This was in addition to an extraordinarily generous pension that, as guaranteed by the LIRR's union contracts, permitted retirement at age fifty and a pension based on the employee's last year's salary, which for the LIRR's senior engineers averaged between $215,000 and $275,000 a year. Those salaries, in turn, had gotten so high—up to three times "normal" salary—because of union rules that permitted, for example, earning four days' wages in a single shift—an accomplishment reached by one retired engineer *thirty times* in his last year.

Oh, and I almost forgot: Every one of these supposedly disabled and retired former employees gets to golf free at any public course. And that's where the *New York Times* found them, generally hitting those fairways and greens twice a week. Well, you have a lot of time to practice your backswing when you're a fifty-year-old retiree living on $170,000 a year.

Think the temptation to game the system is peculiar to New York or railroads? More than two-thirds of the highest-ranking officials of the California Highway Patrol pursue, and receive, disability before their retirement. That retirement, by union contract, is something to which they are entitled at age fifty, along with a pension—before disability payments—of 3 percent of their last year's compensation multiplied by the number of years they've worked. Which means that assistant chiefs who started at age twenty can retire when they're fifty years old at a salary of 90 percent of their last, and highest, paycheck. In New York, a "presumptive disability" law requires that a doctor assume that certain illnesses are job related, which means that firefighters or police officers with something wrong with their lungs qualify for disability even if they have a pack-a-day habit. It's no surprise that 80 percent qualify; one FDNY lieutenant retired in 2001 with an $86,000 annual disability pension after a doctor certified him as asthmatic—even though he is spending his retirement competing in triathlons.

Welcome to the wonderful world of public employee unions.

The unionized portion of the American workforce—less than 12 percent—is less than half of what it was at its 1954 peak of over 28 percent. The reasons are complicated: They include geography (as the U.S. population has shifted to western and southern states, whose history and local laws make them less welcoming to unions) and relative declines in historically unionized industries, particularly manufacturing and mining. But the decline hasn't been the same everywhere. While the percentage of union members in the private sector is now barely 7 percent, public-sector unions have more than picked up the slack. As of this writing, nearly 40 percent of America's public employees are members of unions; the United States Postal Service now has three times as many union employees as the auto industry. And with the most union-friendly president and Senate in decades, that number seems likely to increase.

The attractions of government work to unions (and unions to government work) aren't too difficult to figure out. The typical effect of unionization on wages, which is to inflate the take-home pay of union members somewhere between 10 percent and 30 percent over what their nonunionized colleagues earn, is certainly working pretty well in the public sector: The average government employee not only earns more than he would in a comparable private-sector job,* but he also gets better benefits. And far more job security; as James Sherk of the Heritage Foundation puts it, "The government doesn't have to worry about going bankrupt, and there isn't much competition."

Well, there *is* competition. But it's between different unions to see who can own the biggest share of the public trough. There's the 2.2 million–member Service Employees International Union, for example, which represents local and state government employees. The SEIU felt the wobble in its traditional business earlier than most and changed its name from the Building Service Employees Union in the 1960s† (which is why it still represents hundreds of thousands of janitors and hospital and health-care workers in the private sector).

That same competitive urge has helped the SEIU to become one of the largest unions in the country—and when competitiveness wasn't enough, the SEIU earned a reputation for intimidating workers, tampering with their ballots, and even threatening Latino organizers from a rival union that it would call the INS to get them deported. But it wasn't its tactics that made the SEIU into what the Heritage Foundation calls "President Obama's favorite union"; it was the $85 million it spent in the 2008 campaign—nearly $30 million to support Obama alone. Andy Stern, the former president of the SEIU, actually has the distinction of having been the most frequent visitor to the Obama White House during its first year.

"Blake, have you ever heard the phrase 'setting a fox to guard the chicken coop'?"

---

* A lot more: At the federal level, the average government employee earns 45 percent more than the average private-sector worker with similar duties and qualifications; in Ohio, they earn 34 percent more in total compensation, including wages, benefits, and pension; in Michigan it's 47 percent.

† It is no coincidence that until the 1960s, government employees weren't even allowed to unionize.

"I think so . . ."

"Why wouldn't it be a good idea?"

"Because foxes eat chickens?"

"They do. But what if the fox promised that he wouldn't eat *your* chickens?"

"I don't think I'd trust him so much."

That's one way Blake is more skeptical than the Obama administration, which in March of 2010 named SEIU lawyer Craig Becker to serve on the National Labor Relations Board. Now, there's nothing new about setting foxes to guard the chicken coop when it comes to the NLRB, but Becker is a fox the size of a Bengal tiger. To understand why, you need to know why the number one priority of every union in the country is something called "card check"—a procedure by which a union gets the right to representation if more than half the employees at any site sign a union card—something just as binding as an old-fashioned secret-ballot election.

Now, nothing prevents individual businesses from accepting card check instead of a secret ballot, of course. But there is one big difference between a contract negotiated with a card-check union and one signed by an elected union: Under federal law, after an election, the union's membership can vote to decertify it only after the contract negotiated by that union expires; a union that negotiates a contract via card-check membership can—according to the NLRB, which ruled on this in 2007—still be decertified at any time. Which doesn't happen all that often: Since 2007, card-check unions have been recognized more than 1,100 times. Fifty-four times a vote was demanded, and in fifteen of those elections, the workers voted against the union.

Seems a pretty good batting average. But not good enough for the Obama administration, which has long supported a little bit of legislation called the Employee Free Choice Act, which would make a card-check union just as valid as one elected via secret ballot, a law that is so biased in favor of unions that George McGovern—*George McGovern!*—opposes it. Since most legislators agree with him, the only way to impose card check is via regulation.

Guess who's revisiting the 2007 decision? Craig Becker, who signed a pledge that he wouldn't deal with his former employer at the SEIU—and then said that he had only agreed to recuse himself from business with the SEIU's *locals*. The SEIU's former lawyer sees no problem ruling on issues affecting the *national* union.

Tired of hearing about the SEIU? Well, there's always the 1.4 million–member American Federation of State, County and Municipal Employees, or AFSCME, which spent $87.5 million to support union-friendly candidates in the 2010 midterm elections, more than any other outside interest group, and $10 million *more* than the United States Chamber of Commerce, a favorite bogeyman for Progressive politicians. That's when it's not campaigning for higher state taxes to pay for salaries and pensions that are already higher than those of the average taxpayer. AFSCME is the reason that local government is even more likely to be unionized than federal government—and far more likely to be influenced by unions, which have a lot more direct clout over the reelection prospects of a city council member than a member of the U.S. Senate.

In addition to the wonderful-for-unions phenomenon that governments have no competition and never go out of business is the fact that most government jobs, including police, firefighting, and teaching, are unavoidably labor intensive; unlike with manufacturing automobiles or calculating actuarial tables, it's hard to replace human with machine labor as its cost increases. However, there's another aspect of public employees that makes them even more formidable: The people they're negotiating with are elected officials—and the voters who elect them are the same people with whom they have to agree on wages and pensions. It's bad enough for government to be negotiating with its own employees; it's terrible to negotiate with a bloc of voters as well.*

The results have been predictable. And uniformly bad for every taxpayer who isn't a member of a public-sector union. And the *least* bad outcome is the wage premium now earned by government employees. At the same time that unions have become less and less a part of America's private sector, they have become a bigger and bigger part of the country's campaign-donation machine. Government employee unions contribute more money to congressional candidates than—to pick an example—the total contributed by oil industry political action committees, employees, and executives combined. And those candidates, who are overwhelmingly Democrats, have returned the favor, mortgaging the future of state after state with future pension and health-care obligations to their unionized workforces.

The poster child for this particular time bomb is the state of California, which now contributes more than $7 billion annually to its state pension fund—and is still more than $100 billion behind, in what are technically called "unfunded liabilities": the amount of money that it would take to guarantee those obligations. By any measure, California and dozens of other states are technically bankrupt, entirely because of their long-term debts to their own employees. However, the solution available to bankrupt corporations—renegotiating these debts—isn't open to them because of laws that were essentially written by union staffs to prevent such renegotiation.

Unions are a problem for a free-market economy. Industrial unions are a bigger problem than craft unions. Public-sector unions are a bigger problem than industrial unions. And the biggest problem

---

* Public employees who are forbidden to strike, like most police and firefighters, get an even better deal: They are usually allowed to demand "interest arbitration," in which a third party settles contract disputes, thereby letting local politicians off the hook for the most expensive settlements.

within the public sector is its single largest component—and the one that matters most to the Kernen family: teachers.

The notion that everyone's labor is equal in value to everyone else's is central to the whole idea of unions. In any particular region or company, every machinist, every drill press operator, every truck driver with the same number of years on the job is supposed to be paid the same hourly wage. As a result, unions reward mediocrity—or at least they don't punish it. Just in case you needed reminding, this is the reason that unions are so beloved of liberals and Progressives, who are reflexive in choosing collectivism over individualism. This belief costs the American economy hundreds of billions of dollars annually (and if you add in the money owed to union pension funds, more like trillions).

But at least these costs are "only" money. The belief that one teacher's labor is identical in value to every other's is costing a whole lot more.

"So . . . wait a minute."

"What, Blake?"

"Are you telling me that Mrs. ——— can't get fired?"

"Not unless her boss is willing to spend months in court."

"And she gets paid the same as Miss ———?" (Names withheld on the advice of lawyers.)

"If they've worked the same number of years, then yes."

"That's just crazy."

Crazy, indeed. After decades of research trying to figure out the most important factor in educating kids, the evidence seems pretty clear: It isn't money per pupil or class size. It isn't more rigorous textbooks or more arts and music. In fact, once you control for income and education, and all those other advantages that affluent families give their children, what's left still matters, and what's left is the quality of the teacher. Some second-grade teachers do a consistently great job taking first graders and turning them into third graders. Most do a decent job. And some do a lousy job—year in and year out, with all kinds of kids. If America is serious about improving the education of the next generation of kids—of Blake and Scott and millions like them—there's nothing that would have more impact than just firing the poorest-performing 5 percent of America's primary- and secondary-school teachers.

Only we can't. And the reason is teachers' unions.

The task of firing incompetent teachers is not for the faint of heart, mostly because of the collective bargaining agreements that make firing a teacher, even for the most ridiculous behavior, as hard and as exhausting as changing the mind of an IRS auditor. For years, teachers in the New York City school district who were so bad that even their own principals needed to get them out of the classroom spent months, even years, pulling down full salaries while spending every school day in a "rubber room" in downtown Manhattan.

The Obama administration is so friendly to unions that it is on record supporting card check, whether by legislation or—via Craig Becker—regulation. But that's still not good enough for the National Education Association, which sees the president's support for paying good teachers more than bad teachers and—horror of horrors!—making it possible to actually fire bad teachers as something akin to a crime against humanity.

Part of the reason for teachers' extraordinary job security is the incorporation of something called tenure into union contracts. If the precise meaning of the term is a little fuzzy to you—it was to me—you should remember that it has morphed quite a bit from its origins. Tenure began more than a century ago as the custom of offering what is essentially lifetime job security to the highest-ranking scholars at colleges and universities. It may still have some justification there—the original reason was to guarantee that scholarship would be free of political or economic pressure—though you can certainly find a lot of academics who disagree. But the concept has been redefined in a particularly idiotic way when it is offered to elementary-school teachers as a matter of course after two or three years of work. This has happened in dozens of places, but the one that matters most to me is the state of New Jersey.

From 2000 to 2010, student enrollment in the Garden State grew by 4 percent; during that same period the total number of school employees increased more than three times as much (and we're not alone; New York added fifteen thousand teachers during the same period—when student enrollment *fell* by 121,000). For most of that time, the Kernen family has been sending its children to New Jersey public schools: Blake and Scott both attend schools in the Millburn Township School District, which hasn't had to worry overmuch about either tenure or salaries during the six years that at least one of them has been in school.

But when New Jersey elected a new governor in 2009 and saddled him with a deficit as large as the GDP of Iceland—*before* its bank meltdown—and he started cutting the state budget, New Jersey's schools were a prime candidate.

Governor Chris Christie, who had been elected specifically on the promise to get state spending in general, and education spending in particular, under control, proposed cuts of $800 million in the New Jersey school budget. He did hold out a carrot: If the state's teachers agreed to take a one-year pay freeze and contribute 1.5 percent of their salaries—an average of $65 a month—to medical, dental, and vision benefits (as opposed to the nothing they currently pay), then no cuts would be needed.

Governor Christie is a regular guest on *Squawk Box*, partly because he's smart, mostly because he doesn't mince words. As he told me (and our national audience), the problem with most union benefits is simple arithmetic: "The actuaries tell us that the current system is $34 billion underfunded—and if we made all the payments we're supposed to, in fifteen years it will be *$85 billion* underfunded. I keep telling all those union members who are angry with me that they'll be sending me Christmas cards in ten years thanking me because they'll *have* a pension."

To most New Jersey residents, Christie's offer seemed a reasonable solution, given that we were in the worst recession in decades. To New Jersey's teachers, however, the governor was about as welcome as a smallpox epidemic—and that's how they tried to depict him. Christie then offered the same deal to individual districts (New Jersey has more than six hundred, each with its own administrators, school boards—and union locals), reminding them that if the New Jersey Education Association, which currently demands a little more than $700 a year in dues, agreed to survive without those dues for a year, then *it* could pay for the teachers' insurance. They refused.

I told him that the unions would eventually beat him into submission. His response: "It doesn't work anymore, Joe. No one thinks that teachers must have free health care from the day they're hired until the day they die. And no one thinks that has anything to do with educating our children. No kid is going to come home and tell you, 'I can't study because my teacher has to pay 1.5 percent for health benefits.'"

Our own school district was one of the ones that decided to maintain teacher salaries, with their guaranteed raises for 2010, instead of renegotiating. As a result, some thirty staff members—all of them nonunion—have been fired.

Blake doesn't understand everything about unions. But in the one area of her life where she deals with adults in their workplaces, she sees their most important aspect, which is to take care of themselves at the expense of everyone else.

Long ago, when Blake was very small, I remember reading her a story. The details are a little fuzzy, but I remember it was about a sleigh riding through a blizzard, pursued by wolves. Every so often, the people in the sleigh would pick out a passenger and throw that passenger out of the sleigh, in the hope that the wolves would take him or her, but not them. I have no doubt that the sleigh was driven by union teamsters.

It's sometimes easy to forget that a free-market economy depends on a free market in labor, just like everything else. I'm no purist about this: America is rich enough to afford some level of price-fixing by labor unions, particularly those that provide something valuable, like a guarantee that your electrician knows how to keep your house from burning down when you turn on a light switch.

So I'll pay a little extra for that union label—sometimes. But that's my choice. When unions insist on laws that require everyone— Democrat or Republican, Progressive or free-market conservative— working for a particular company or industry or, worst of all, for the government itself, to join up, and especially to kick in money for political candidates they may despise, well, I *choose* not to.

CHAPTER 10

December 2010: Lies, D***ed Lies, and the Opinion Pages

One of the aspects of this project for which Penelope and I will have to answer in the next life is our decision to spend eighteen months—from the inauguration of Barack Obama in January 2009 to the middle of 2010— discussing the daily editorials in the New York Times *and the* Wall Street Journal *with Blake. Our goal wasn't punishment, though it's possible Blake might disagree. The idea, instead, was to see how the same economic story or public debate was handled by the two papers. Our only defense was that there is no better place to observe the battle lines in the fight over the future of free-market capitalism; from climate-change policy to the regulation of the nation's financial system to the "reform" of the health-insurance industry.*

Someday Blake will forgive us.

On July 24, 2004, then-Senator Barack Obama gave a speech to the Democratic National Convention and a national television audience. For those who have forgotten 2004—when unemployment was still under 5.5 percent, the annual deficit was still "only" $668 billion, and more than $10 trillion of wealth hadn't yet vanished from America's net worth—the speech in question was the one in which the future president reminded us that "there is not a liberal America and a conservative America."

On November 2, 2010—the day of the midterm elections that "refudiated"* two years of Progressive rule and turned the House of Representatives over to the Republican Party by the biggest margin in more than sixty years—the American voter disagreed. In fact, disagreement on every aspect of the Obama presidency kind of defined the election—including the way it was explained.

One editorial put it this way:

> The Republicans spent months fanning Americans' anger over the economy and fear of "big government," while offering few ideas of their own. Exit polls indicated that they had succeeded in turning out their base, and that the Democrats had failed to rally their own.

The problem?

> Mr. Obama needs to break his habits of neglecting his base voters and of sitting on the sidelines and allowing others to shape the debate. He needs to do a much better job of stiffening the spines of his own party's leaders.
>
> "Election 2010," *New York Times*, November 3, 2010

According to the *New York Times*, the election

---

* Ever since former governor Palin coined the word, I have been using it on *Squawk Box* to combine "refutation" and "repudiation"—simultaneously dismantling and denouncing a position. In November 2010, the *Oxford American Dictionary* picked it as the word of the year.

was hardly an order from the American people to
discard the progress of the last two years and start
over again. . . . The Republican victory was impressive and definitive, although voters who made it happen were hardly spread evenly across the electorate.
The victory was built largely on the heavy turnout of
older blue-collar white men, most in the South or
the rusting Midwest.

"Sorting Out the Election," *New York Times*, November 4, 2010

Not exactly. The *Wall Street Journal* pointed out:

Throughout the Northeast and Midwest, Republicans regained House seats that pundits had declared
were lost to a GOP that had supposedly become
merely a Southern party.

"The Four-Year Majority," *Wall Street Journal*, November 3, 2010

There was even disagreement about the president's performance
at his news conference the day after what he called the "shellacking"
his party had just experienced:

Mr. Obama was on target when he said voters howled
in frustration at the slow pace of economic recovery
and job creation.

"Sorting Out the Election," *New York Times*, November 4, 2010

In his press conference yesterday, Mr. Obama did not
sound like someone ideologically chastened by the
rout of his fellow Democrats. He said he felt "bad"
for so many careers cut short, and that he was thinking about his own role in the defeat. But he rejected

the thought that his own policies were to blame, save
for the fact that they haven't—yet—produced an economic recovery robust enough to make everything
else he did popular.

"The Boehner Evolution," *Wall Street Journal*, November 5, 2010

As the Progressive reaction to the midterm elections of 2010
showed, liberal America may still be alive and kicking—for a while,
anyway—but it's pretty much blind to reality. An electoral thump-
ing that was unmistakably a referendum on Progressive policies was,
to Progressives, a failure of timing. Or communication. Or apathy on
the part of other Progressives. Or anything but what it was. And this
was true not only to the readers of the *Huffington Post* and *Mother
Jones* but to the readers of America's newspaper of record, the *New
York Times*.

The *Times*'s influence is so wide, in fact, that the only comparable
daily newspaper is the bible of American business, the *Wall Street
Journal*, which actually shares a lot of its competitor's characteristics.
Both win Pulitzer Prizes by the truckload. Both are at the top of the
career ladder for every aspiring journalist in the country. Both are
based in Manhattan, for gosh sakes.

But when it comes to every public-policy debate, they might as
well be in two different galaxies. If the *Times* thinks a particular
tax is too low, you *know* that the *Journal* thinks it's too high. If
the *Times* hates a Supreme Court decision, the *Journal* loves it. If the
Times endorses Smith for dogcatcher, you can bet the *Journal* is back-
ing Jones.

And so is the Kernen family. I read both newspapers every day,
and you've probably already guessed which one I think understands
the way the world works. As regular viewers of *Squawk Box* know, I'm
no great fan of the *Times* editorial pages. If I had to imagine a particularly awful way to spend eternity, it would be having to read
Frank Rich's column every day, rather than just on Sunday. You can't

even explain his presence by the Progressive fondness for highly credentialed elites; the man whom the *Times* pays to write fifteen hundred words on economic policy every week was formerly a theater critic, for heaven's sake.

On the other hand, not only does the *Journal* have a bunch of really smart reporters who understand every aspect of business and the American economy, but its editorials are practically a textbook of free-market philosophy. In fact, I can honestly say that this book owes as much to the last two pages of the *Journal*'s first section as it does to anything else.

Ask any Progressive, and he'll tell you all about the science of climate change. Men who never took a chemistry class after the tenth grade will bend your ear on convection models, climate forcing, or the medieval warm period. Women who—maybe—took a "science for poets" class in college will go on and on about the kinetic theory of gases, Arctic sea ice, and isotherms. And sooner or later, one of them will mention the Nobel Prize awarded to the Intergovernmental Panel on Climate Change and (of course) former vice president Al Gore.

Now, I don't mean to sound like a science snob, but before I joined the investment world I spent a good many years in laboratories working with and for some of the world's best experimental researchers. And I do know that anything as complicated as the world's climate is not the kind of thing that can be understood by watching a one-hundred-minute-long documentary, even if it has Al Gore in it. (I also know one thing for sure about science: It isn't about "truth," inconvenient or not. There is no such thing as "settled science." Or "incontrovertible evidence." If anyone tries to tell you there is, feel free to back away, slowly, with your hand firmly on your wallet.)

Even so, it isn't really the *science* of climate change that generates all the controversy. The thing that matters—that really divides Progressive thinking from, well, common sense—is climate *policy*. More specifically, the economics of climate policy. And this is why the world's climate looks so much different from the *New York Times* offices on Forty-second Street than it does less than five miles south, at the *Wall Street Journal*.

Take the villainous substance that is at the heart of all climate change debates: carbon dioxide, or CO_2.*

Carbon dioxide is not exactly an exotic substance. Almost every organism on the planet either produces it or consumes it; the cycle of life itself depends on plants turning CO_2 into carbohydrates and animals turning carbohydrates back into CO_2. It's not much of a stretch to say that without carbon dioxide, life as we know it wouldn't exist.

"Blake?"

"Yes, Dad?"

"What do you know about carbon dioxide—CO_2?"

"Like in the song?"

"Song?"

"The song we learned at summer school: 'Unlike me and you / Plants need CO_2 / That lets off oxygen / That keeps us from turning blue / Every plant can do this fundamental process / And we can call this photosynthesis.'"

"Yes, Blake. Just like that."

Life depends on CO_2—oops, I meant to write carbon—for more than just photosynthesis. Every instant, the sun radiates a huge amount of energy, some of which hits earth. That energy comes in different flavors: the kind we can see—visible light—passes through

---

* Or as virtually every Progressive calls it, "carbon." The transformation of carbon dioxide—a colorless, tasteless, and quite harmless gas—into "carbon," with all its echoes of the dirty stuff that is dug out of the ground and coats the lungs with dust, is one of the greatest PR triumphs since the days of P. T. Barnum.

CO_2, but a large amount of energy that we *feel*, mostly in the form of heat, is absorbed. The result, due to this "greenhouse effect," is that earth is warm enough to support life. For living things, carbon dioxide is, by any measure, a good thing.

Now, it is certainly possible to have too much of a good thing, and the entire climate-change controversy is built around the contention that CO_2 is a really good thing when its percentage of earth's atmosphere is 0.03 percent but a disaster when it is 0.04 percent. Accept this, and you have joined the "consensus."

Here's how you get there:

Step 1: Carbon dioxide is a "greenhouse" gas. No argument.

Step 2: Industrial civilization has produced more atmospheric carbon dioxide than would have been present if, for example, humanity were still dependent on muscle and waterpower. Since CO_2 and water are the result of the chemical reaction that occurs whenever a fuel that contains carbon is burned, also no argument.

Step 3: Globally, temperatures are rising. Plenty of argument here, mostly about the magnitude of the rise. It turns out to be very hard to measure worldwide temperature, since it can, for example, be hotter in one place this year than it was last year, while cooler elsewhere. However, for the sake of argument, let's accept that it is rising.

Step 4: It's rising a lot. This is where the argument starts to show some tatters; the Intergovernmental Panel on Climate Change, which is the body usually used to "prove" the dangers of global climate change, estimates that if current trends continue, the worldwide temperature will rise somewhere between three and five degrees Fahrenheit by the year 2100. This matters—but how much? In the long history of the planet, this is barely noticeable (and even in the northeastern United States, where the Kernen family lives, a December day that is 45 degrees rather than 42 degrees isn't going to make headlines).

Also, while such a worldwide increase in temperature does have some serious costs attached to it, mostly in the form of rising sea levels, it also has some benefits. Places way too cold for agriculture today would be available, and those doomsayers worried about feeding a few billion people in the face of a "climate disaster" should also know that crop yields are expected to *increase* by more than 10 percent because of increased amounts of carbon dioxide—which plants "breathe"—in the atmosphere.

Step 5: We need to stop the temperature rise, no matter what the cost. This is where the argument really unravels. That predicted temperature increase—from the IPCC, remember—has been estimated to cost a bit more than $20 trillion, which is a huge sum of money. But it's a huge sum of money *a hundred years from now*. While the cost of avoiding that temperature rise is the equivalent of $14 trillion *right now*.

Think about it. Pick door number one, and you get to spend $14 today. Or select door number two, and spend $20 a century from now, when you (or rather, Blake's great-grandchildren) will be ten times richer than you are today.

Behind door number one is the *New York Times*.

Take, for example, the small matter of whether CO_2 is a dangerous substance. Back in 2007, a federal judge ruled that the Environmental Protection Agency was required to decide whether carbon dioxide was something that "threatens public health and welfare." The "endangerment finding" that resulted was tabled by the Bush administration but greeted by the *New York Times* with the kind of enthusiasm usually reserved for the discovery of a winning lottery ticket in your sock drawer.

Here's what the *Times* editorial page had to say about the endangerment finding:

The mere prospect of regulation has inspired something approaching panic. . . . The House, in an otherwise admirable climate change bill, included a provision restricting the E.P.A.'s authority to control emissions.

This is utterly wrongheaded. The Supreme Court ruled two years ago that the E.P.A. has clear authority under the Clean Air Act to regulate greenhouse gases. It should be retained as both a goad and a backstop.

There is one obvious way to keep the E.P.A. from having to use this authority on a broad scale. And that is for Congress to pass a credible and comprehensive bill requiring economy wide cuts in emissions.

"The Endangerment Finding," *New York Times*, December 8, 2009

This has to be read twice to fully appreciate it: The United States House of Representatives—which was, in 2009, still firmly in the hands of the Democratic Party—having already voted to restrict the EPA's authority, is told by the *Times* that the best way to keep the EPA from requiring massive cuts in CO_2 emissions is for *Congress* to require them first.

"Blake?"

"Yes?"

"What would you say if I told you that your school wanted to require all fifth graders to go to sleep at seven thirty?"

"That's not my bedtime!"

"I know. But what if Mommy and I told the school that we didn't want them to decide about your bedtime, and they told us that the best way to keep them from setting bedtime at seven thirty was for us to do it."

"I'd say that was blackmail."

The *Wall Street Journal* agrees:

> This reckless "endangerment finding" is a political ultimatum: The many Democrats wary of levelling huge new costs on their constituents must surrender, or else the EPA's carbon police will inflict even worse consequences.
>
> "An Inconvenient Democracy," *Wall Street Journal*,
> December 8, 2009

Progressives are very comfortable using the courts and the EPA to threaten Congress into transforming the entire American economy—and make no mistake about that: *everything* that produces or demands power depends on burning carbon-based fuels—partly because of their fundamental inability to compare costs and benefits: Global warming is just *bad*, so asking how much it costs to eliminate it is like asking how much you would spend to save a life. But even more so, I think, it's their love for solutions that have the endorsement of elites—in this case, the scientific community.

The elevation of climate scientists—the *right* climate scientists, of course—to the position once occupied by high priests of mystery religions is sort of understandable. It's hard enough to find people with a basic understanding of physics and chemistry, to say nothing of the interdisciplinary clutter of experts needed to investigate an area like climate. Add to that the fact that none of these people's conclusions can be experimentally tested and must therefore be made using computer models and historical data (this is also true of economics—

whose track record in predicting booms and busts is not exactly encouraging) and you have a very nearly perfect storm: a complicated scientific subject in which even professionals are compelled to rely on other professionals working in fields that they don't understand; in which no one can test hypotheses experimentally; and in which conclusions depend on tiny changes in the underlying data. High priests never had it so good.

On the other hand, one reason that science gets such respect in a modern technological society is the belief that it is performed by honorable people who report things the way they see them. This doesn't mean that we have to count on any individual scientist to find the holes in his or her pet theory; but it does mean that we can rely on the entire community of scientists in a given field to be critical of themselves and to report their findings honestly.

Uh-oh.

The scandal that would, soon enough, be called Climategate broke in November 2009, when a computer at the Climate Research Unit (CRU) at the University of East Anglia was hacked, and thousands of e-mails and documents written by the world's best-known, and most alarmist, climate scientists appeared on the Internet. The portrait they painted wasn't exactly the picture of honesty. Phil Jones, director of the CRU, wrote (about a request for the raw data on which he based his predictions), "I think I'll delete the file rather than give it to anyone." Writing to Michael Mann, a like-minded researcher at Penn State, he said: "Mike, Can you delete any e-mails you may have had re AR4 [the IPCC's Fourth Assessment Report]?" Writing to Eugene Wahl of the National Oceanic and Atmospheric Administration: "Try and change the received date! Don't give those skeptics something to amuse themselves with."

Just destroying and withholding data wasn't enough for Professor Mann, who was so disturbed by a critical article appearing in one journal that he suggested, "I think we have to stop considering *Cli-*

mate Research as a legitimate peer-reviewed journal. . . . Perhaps we should encourage our colleagues in the climate research community to no longer submit to, or cite papers in, this journal."

The *Wall Street Journal*, quite rightly, saw this as a huge problem:

> The response from the defenders of Mr. Mann and his circle has been that even if they did disparage doubters and exclude contrary points of view, theirs is still the best climate science. The proof for this is circular. It's the best, we're told, because it's the most-published and most-cited—in that same peer-reviewed literature. The public has every reason to ask why they felt the need to rig the game if their science is as indisputable as they claim.
>
> "Rigging a Climate Consensus," *Wall Street Journal*,
> November 27, 2009

Not, however, the *New York Times*:

> It is important that scientists behave professionally and openly. It is also important not to let one set of purloined e-mail messages undermine the science and the clear case for action, in Washington and in Copenhagen.
>
> "The Climate Change E-Mail," *New York Times*,
> December 6, 2009

And when, in July 2010, Professor Mann—the creator of the famous "hockey stick" graph, which showed a steady planetary temperature over a nine-hundred-year period, followed by a sudden upward turn beginning with the Industrial Revolution—was, in the words of the *New York Times*, "exonerated" by his university (he wasn't; he was vindicated on three of the four charges—mostly on the grounds that even though Phil Jones had clearly asked him to destroy a raft of e-mails, there was no evidence that Dr. Mann ever got around to it), the *Times* wrote,

> Perhaps now we can put the manufactured contro-
> versy known as Climategate behind us and turn to
> the task of actually doing something about global
> warming.
>
> "A Climate Change Corrective," *New York Times*, July 9, 2010

In other words, a university panel proved that Professor Mann didn't manufacture data by finding a "consensus" among other climate scientists on the same data—published in the journals that Professor Mann and his colleagues in the climate science community agreed not to boycott.

It took the *Wall Street Journal* to reveal the reason why:

> Consider the cash that Michael Mann . . . has helped
> pull for Penn State University. In 2000, before Mr.
> Mann joined the faculty, the university banked $20.4
> million in research funding for environmental sci-
> ences. By 2007, two years after he came on board,
> Penn State counted more than $55 million a year for
> environmental research, much of it government
> funded. . . . The gusher of money that has flowed
> into climate research does not, by itself, impeach the
> conclusions reached by the scientists. But it does
> make clear just how much their professional fortunes
> became tied to the notion of climate catastrophe.
>
> "The Economics of Climate Change," *Wall Street Journal*,
> November 30, 2009

Maybe, in the end, climate scientists really *do* know something about economic costs and benefits—to themselves, anyway.

What they don't know is the danger of "consensus" science. When Blake was taking a science class during the summer of 2010, one of her projects was a simple lab on cell biology, describing what she saw through a microscope. I asked her whether anyone had seen anything different, and she told me that was impossible: Everyone needed to see the same thing when they looked through the microscope. If anyone saw something different, they were just wrong. They *had* to be.

On climate change, the real difference between the *Times* and the *Journal* wasn't that they disagreed over science, or even policy. Reading the two papers' editorials with Blake in mind, I realized that what separated them was that the *Journal* took the side of optimism: that the best way to deal with the costs of global climate change, whatever they were, was to increase prosperity. The *Times* stood for fear, advocating just about anything that would even *symbolically* reduce the world's production of CO_2—if they had been fully implemented for ninety years, the Kyoto Protocols, a favorite of the *New York Times* editorial board, would have reduced global temperatures by only a tenth of one degree Fahrenheit—at a cost of $250 billion a year.

If you want your children to fear the future, let them read the *Times* editorials. Otherwise, well, you get the point.

I've noticed that people tend to believe that if there must be legislation, the legislators should be people like them. Politicians already think that politicians do a pretty good job (though, as the 2010 elections showed, nonpoliticians *also* think they would do a better one); scientists would like to see more scientists writing laws and statutes. If you know any doctors, you will, sooner or later, hear one of them bemoan the fact that "the world is run by people who couldn't get into medical school." And this is why, against all evidence, movie stars continue to think they have something useful to say about legislation to reduce world hunger, for example.

So it isn't actually all that surprising that business professionals in general, and those in the finance industry in particular, thought that they might have done a better job at financial regulatory reform than the United States Congress managed to do with the Dodd-Frank Wall Street Reform and Consumer Protection Act.*

The financial regulatory reform package was a predictable response to the crisis of 2008 and subsequent recession. The original objectives of revising America's financial regulation laws were

1. to consolidate and streamline the different agencies that were already responsible for regulating banks, mortgage companies, the stock market, and so on;
2. to create a new agency responsible for the protection of consumers of financial products; and
3. to restock the toolbox regulatory agencies use to deal with financial crises.

In the end the act created not just a new Bureau of Consumer Financial Protection but also a Financial Stability Oversight Council and an Office of Financial Research. If this seems contrary to objective number one, welcome to the world of regulation and please go to chapter 7.

The overriding goal was to create an early-warning system for any problems that presented a risk to the entire financial system (rather than to any one institution) and to avoid the risk of taxpayers having to bail out banks, insurance companies, and investment firms that had become "too big too fail." The attempt, according to the summary prepared by the law firm Davis Polk on July 21, 2010, resulted in 243 new rules, required the production of 67 separate studies, and mandated the regular publication of 22 different reports.

And because this massive new law was written by politicians,

---

* The formal name for the statute signed by President Obama on July 21, 2010, is "An Act to Promote the Financial Stability of the United States by Improving Accountability and Transparency in the Financial System, to End 'Too Big to Fail,' to Protect the American Taxpayer by Ending Bailouts, to Protect Consumers from Abusive Financial Services Practices, and for Other Purposes." Washington doesn't do concise.

there's a lot more politics in it than economics (or common sense). Consider, for example, the case of Fannie Mae and Freddie Mac—the Federal National Mortgage Association and the Federal Home Loan Mortgage Corporation—two enterprises chartered by the federal government to promote loans for the purchase of homes.

Though their histories are complicated beyond tedium and include the on-again-off-again fiction that one or the other was a sorta-kinda private corporation and the other a kinda-sorta government agency, the fundamental reason for both GSEs (government-sponsored enterprises—don't you love the acronyms?) is to promote the ability of people to secure home loans. They do this by buying and selling loans in what is known as a "secondary mortgage market" (and by guaranteeing repayment in return for fees on mortgage loans that they repackage into securities).

The idea is to promote home ownership because of the widespread belief that home ownership is a good thing, making for more stable communities and more engaged citizens.* However, the people who tend to need the most help in financing loans also tend to be the ones who are least able to pay those loans back.

"Dad?"

"Yes, Blake?"

"What's a mortgage?"

"It's a sort of loan, Blake. People who want to own houses usually don't have enough cash to just buy them, so they borrow money from someone else, like a bank, promising to pay back the money or else give up the house."

"If the bank wanted the house, why wouldn't it just buy it?"

"The bank doesn't want the house. They want the buyer to pay back the money with interest."

---

* This is the same logic that allows homeowners to deduct the interest on mortgages from their income tax.

"How do they know that the buyer will pay the money?"

"Well, they're supposed to see if you have a good history of paying money back when it's borrowed. And they're supposed to make sure that you earn enough money to pay the money back."

"*Supposed* to?"

Exactly. Beginning in the 1990s, both Fannie Mae and Freddie Mac were regularly and successfully pressured by the federal government to buy more of the loans given to people who didn't qualify for "prime" interest loans. Their huge investment in so-called subprime loans, more than any other single factor, led to a huge crash in housing prices; when people buy stuff they can't afford, they tend to stop paying for it, which meant that the supply of housing quickly outstripped demand. The price? In 2009 the Congressional Budget Office estimated the cost of rescuing the two GSEs from their mistakes at $238 billion.

> If there is a better example of what happens when government allocates resources against the "judgment" of the market, I don't know what it is. As a result, you would think that reform of Fannie and Freddie would be a prime objective of the Dodd-Frank bill. You would be wrong. The eighty-five-page-long "white paper" produced by the Treasury Department, which documented the need for regulatory reform back in June of 2009, named America's banks as the parties responsible for the housing crisis, but "the only mention of Fannie Mae and Freddie Mac is a placeholder paragraph noting that reform of those housing giants will come later."
>
> "Hope Versus Financial Experience," *Wall Street Journal*,
> June 19, 2009

It never did:

> [The] financial reform [bill] runs to 1,300 pages
> but lacks a single sentence on how to reform Fannie
> Mae or Freddie Mac. Actually, it's worse than that.
> One provision could make Fannie and Freddie even
> more dominant in the business of mortgage-backed
> securities. . . . It works like this: One provision in the
> bill intends to encourage lenders to be more careful
> about the loans they make by requiring them to re-
> tain more of the risk when they sell these loans to
> investors. Specifically, banks that originate loans and
> then sell them will need to retain 5% of the credit
> risk. . . . The result would be less credit available—
> except there appears to be a way around this rule.
> Procuring a Fannie or Freddie guarantee removes
> the transaction's credit risk.
>
> "A Favor for Fannie Mae," *Wall Street Journal*, March 22, 2010

This didn't represent a big problem for the *New York Times*, however:

> Meanwhile, the administration should investigate
> ways to facilitate more refinancing [through] Fannie
> Mae and Freddie Mac, the government-controlled
> mortgage companies.
>
> "Housing on the Brink," *New York Times*, September 2, 2010)

There are a few reasons why the thousand-plus pages of the financial-reform bill pay so little attention to the actions of Fannie and Freddie. The first one is that the Frank of Dodd-Frank is Mas-sachusetts congressman Barney Frank, who in 2000 called concerns about Fannie and Freddie "overblown," claiming there was "no federal liability whatsoever," and in 2002 said, "I do not regard Fannie Mae and Freddie Mac as problems. I regard them as assets," and even in 2008 was still defending them, saying, "The private sector got us into this mess. . . . The government has to get us out of it."*

But the bigger reason is the predictable one: Progressive thinking *always* prefers a government solution to a market one. And so (surprise!) does the *New York Times*. In fact, the *Times* used up so much of the milk of human kindness in support of Fannie and Freddie that it was fresh out when it came to the paychecks earned by people in the financial-services industry.

Now, I admit that it's a little hard to generate great gobs of sympathy for people who are paid the kind of bonuses that have become standard operating procedure in the banking, insurance, and investment businesses. But the principle of executive compensation is only one of the dozens of economic subjects about which the *New York Times* has an opinion. A wrongheaded opinion. More than anyone else, the *Times* has been leading the charge to restrict the amount of money that banks and other institutions pay their senior employees, because the banks were recipients of the huge loans associated with the various aspects of the 2008 and 2009 bailouts.

The loans themselves had come with a lot of strings attached, including restrictions on compensation. This was one of the reasons that so many of the banks receiving federal loans were so eager to repay them and so get out from under the pay guidelines (and, by the way, one of the reasons that the U.S. government actually made a *profit* on the Troubled Asset Relief Program that stands, as of this writing, somewhere north of $50 billion).

But the idea that the federal government needs to "rein in" overly rich pay packages survived loan repayment; in the words of the *Times* editorial board:

---

* In all fairness, by August 2010, Congressman Frank was actually calling for the abolition of Fannie and Freddie and even admitting that maybe "everyone shouldn't be a homeowner." Better a few trillion dollars late than never, I guess.

Ideally, banks would be free to compensate employees as they saw fit. But that must be accompanied by reforms that ensure that banks can no longer profit from primarily speculative activities.

New York Times, August 1, 2009

Which prompted this back-and-forth with Blake:

"Blake?"

"Yes, Daddy?"

"Did you read the e-mail I sent?"

Silence.

"Blake?"

"I read most of it."

"What'd you think?"

"Well, the guys at the *Times* don't want us to pay the banks, and the guys at the *Journal* do."

"Not the banks. The bankers."

"Right. Bankers."

"What do you think about that?"

"Well, I didn't really understand it."

"What didn't you understand?

"Well, in the part I read, the guys at the *Times* thought these bankers were paid too much, and they didn't want us to pay them. But we're not paying them, are we?"

The political appeal of this is obvious; its economic justification is about as obvious as capping the pay of Tina Fey because *30 Rock* is broadcast over public airwaves and regulated cable systems. For example:

Fed officials get the basic idea, that bankers' compensation must be structured in a way that makes them think twice before they place bets that could lead their institutions (and the rest of us) over the cliff again. . . . The Fed says it has also begun a review of current payment practices at the 28 banks and will veto payment structures it does not like. It must be ready to impose more specific restrictions if bankers game the system.

"The State of Financial Reform," *New York Times*,
October 25, 2009

Luckily, the *Wall Street Journal* sees that this particular emperor isn't wearing any clothes:

In most of Europe, the notion that "bank pay did it" is now settled truth. Nicolas Sarkozy wants a pay czar to set compensation levels at French banks. Angela Merkel, up for re-election this weekend, is campaigning against banker bonuses. The Federal Reserve is now joining the act with a proposal to regulate pay structures as a way to police safety and soundness and contain systemic risk. Governments can't get incentives right most of the time in their own policies. So the idea that regulators can better align banker incentives than a competitive marketplace fails the laugh test.

"Extraordinary Popular Delusions," *Wall Street Journal*,
September 23, 2009

But compensation is actually a sideshow in the battle over regulation of the financial-services industry. The main event and the centerpiece of the Dodd-Frank bill was the creation of a new Bureau of Consumer Financial Protection, and needless to say, the *Times* and the *Journal* saw the issues a little, well, differently:

> The new consumer financial protection bureau established in the bill is a milestone, not only for its intent and power to rectify lending abuses, but because it will institutionalize the insight that the safety and soundness of banks cannot—and should not—be measured by profitability alone, but by the impact that bank practices ultimately may have on consumers.
>
> "Congress Passes Financial Reform," *New York Times*, July 15, 2010

> The bureau would have broad power to set the terms of financial products and services, labeling as abusive whatever officials . . . dislike, and paving the way for large new litigation costs. This bureau would barely touch Wall Street, which doesn't oppose it in any case, but it would slam small banks, car dealers and others that extend credit. **The entire point of the bureau is to put politicians in charge of allocating credit**. (Emphasis added.)
>
> "Son of Sarbox," *Wall Street Journal*,
> April 21, 2010

As I said, politicians—or, at least, Progressive politicians—know who should be in charge: them, or at least the regulators they appoint.

It's not just that the *New York Times* loves economic regulation by "experts." The financial industry is hugely complicated, and if you're going to have any regulation at all, expertise isn't the worst qualification I can think of. It's pretty scary, however, that their idea of an expert is someone like Elizabeth Warren, a—wait for it—professor at Harvard Law School and a career academic and the *Times*'s favorite candidate to be director of the new Consumer Financial Protection Bureau, as it is now known. You might think that the best person to run the bureau would be someone with a background in banking or finance; but if so, you're probably reading the *Wall Street Journal* anyway.

There are areas where it is easy to be a free-market advocate, areas where the sheer, unadulterated idiocy of Progressive ideology makes a slam-dunk case for free-market capitalism. And not just an ordinary slam dunk: a slam dunk by Shaquille O'Neal over a bunch of Girl Scouts. Like, for example, the Patient Protection and Affordable Care Act, which was signed into law by President Obama on March 23, 2010.

The Progressive effort to make the national government responsible for the nation's health care (or at least its health insurance) is as old as Progressivism itself; it was one of the promises on which Theodore Roosevelt ran for president on the original Progressive Party ticket. He lost. His cousin, FDR, attempted to make the federal responsibility a part of the original Social Security legislation. He lost, too. Harry Truman in 1949; Richard Nixon in 1972; Bill Clinton in 1993. Lost, lost, lost.

Got to give them credit for persistence.

By the time the Obama administration stepped up to the plate, health care—doctors, pharmaceuticals, hospitals, insurers—accounted for roughly one-sixth of the entire American economy: more than $2 trillion. America spends a lot on its health care, but it gets a lot in return. The free-market component of that trillion-dollar business had produced a steady stream of near-miraculous innovations, from antiretroviral drugs to stereotactic neurosurgery to PET scans. Free-market research and development had lowered infant mortality, extended life span, and transformed the practice of medicine. Procedures that twenty years ago would have taken hours to perform in an operating room were now being done in doctors' offices; knee surgeries that had years-long recovery times (if patients ever really recovered) now had patients running marathons weeks later.

Of course, it needed to be fixed.

Luckily, the incoming administration had a model in mind for the way to fix it. In 2006 the Commonwealth of Massachusetts, under its governor, Republican Mitt Romney, had enacted its own health-care reform, which promised to insure every resident of the state—at no cost to its poorest residents, at a heavily subsidized cost for others. By March 2009, when President Obama announced his intention to tackle the subject, the Massachusetts experience was a clear example . . . of something.

The *Times* saw it this way:

> Four years after Massachusetts enacted its ambitious health care reform, the state has achieved its goal: covering most of the uninsured without seriously straining its budget.
>
> "Reform and Massachusetts," *New York Times*, April 21, 2010

It's not so surprising that the editors of the *New York Times* were able to find evidence that the Massachusetts plan was not only working but doing so "without seriously straining its budget." Psychologists call the tendency to see only the data that confirms preconceptions a "confirmation bias," and it was pretty clear that the *Times* had a ton of preconceptions about not just government enterprises in general but government-run health care in particular. The *Times* opinion on such matters was, well, predictable.

But as the late Senator Daniel Patrick Moynihan used to say, everyone is entitled to his own opinion, but not his own facts. Which is what the *Wall Street Journal* was ready to point out:

> Although Mr. Romney promised that his plan would lower costs, the liberal Commonwealth Fund reports that Massachusetts insurance costs have climbed anywhere from 21% to 46% faster than the U.S. av-

erage since 2005. Employer-sponsored premiums are
now the highest in the nation.

"RomneyCare Revisited," *Wall Street Journal*, January 21, 2010

Of course, the *Times* wasn't just cheerleading for the plan based
on the delusional solvency of the Massachusetts plan, though it's hard
to miss, once again, the chronic inability of Progressives to add up a
column of figures twice and get the same result. As always, the real
attraction is the belief that the best possible health-care system is one
that forbids the squalid search for profit.

The real objective—of the *Times*, a whole lot of the Democratic
Party, and the president himself—was a single-payer system: one in
which *all* medical care is government run and financed. However,
there was, and is, such huge opposition to such a Canadian-style
system that Progressives (outside of predictable places like Cambridge
and Berkeley) apparently decided that their best strategy was misdi-
rection: If they couldn't take over the entire $2 trillion industry at
first, maybe they could do so at last, by what became known as a
"public option" that would "compete" with private insurance.

The essential idea of the public option was incoherent from the
beginning. If people were offered a government-run health-insurance
plan that was neither better nor cheaper than private insurance, they
would have no reason to choose it; on the other hand, the only way
to make it either better or cheaper was to subsidize it . . . which is sort
of the opposite of competition.

"Blake?"

"Yes, Dad?"

"Do you know the difference between private school and public
school?"

"Dad. I'm in fifth grade, for gosh sakes."

"So you do know?"

"Of course. Private school costs a lot more."

"What if they were the same price?"

"Then everybody would go to private school, wouldn't they?"

Yup. Blake's school—a public one, as of this writing, anyway—isn't any cheaper to operate than a private one. But it is "free," which is another way of saying it is paid for by taxes. It doesn't, in any real sense, compete with private schools on price, and the existence of public schools doesn't get them to keep their prices down nearly as much as the existence of other *private* schools. This aspect of the "public option" in education, however, was lost on the editorial board of the *Times*:

> We strongly support inclusion of a public option—the bigger and stronger the better. That is the best way to give consumers more choices, inject more competition into insurance markets, hold down the cost of insurance policies, and save money for the federal budget.
>
> "The Public Plan, Continued," *New York Times*, October 18, 2009

Or maybe not. Here's the *Journal*:

> A public program won't compete in a way that any normal business would recognize. As an entitlement, Congress's creation will enjoy potentially unlimited access to the Treasury, without incurring the risks or hedging against losses that private carriers do. As people gravitate to "free" or heavily subsidized care, the inevitably explosive costs will be covered in part with increased outlays to keep premiums artificially low or even offer extra benefits. . . . A public option is the beginning of the end of private health insurance.
>
> "The End of Private Health Insurance," *Wall Street Journal*,
> April 13, 2009

In the end, the Affordable Care Act—don't you love the way these laws get their names?—didn't include a public option. The Progressive impulse, however, was still alive and kicking. Deprived of the carrot of what they believed would be low-cost health care paid for by taxes (which are always charged to the most productive members of society), they resorted to a stick: a requirement that every American buy insurance.

Even for Progressives, this was groundbreaking. There had never been a law that required anyone to buy anything at all, just for the privilege of breathing; even their favorite example—the requirement that drivers purchase auto insurance—was still a matter of choice: If you want to drive on public roads, you have to have insurance; if you don't want to, you don't have to.

The *New York Times* saw this as a "fundamental question":

> If Congress approves health care reform, virtually all Americans will be required to buy health insurance or pay a penalty. That raises a fundamental question . . .

Could it be? Did the *Times* actually recognize some limit on the legitimacy of the federal government in demanding such a requirement? Uh, no:

> . . . a fundamental question: Will the policies be affordable?
>
> "Mandates and Affordability," *New York Times*, November 1, 2009

No, the "fundamental question" is not affordability; it's *legality*. Here's the *Journal*:

> The centerpiece of the Obama-Baucus plan is a decree that everyone purchase heavily regulated insurance

policies or else pay a penalty. This government mandate would require huge subsidies as well as brute
force to get anywhere near the goal of universal
coverage. . . . Everyone would be forced to buy these
government-approved policies, whether or not they
suit their needs or budget. Families would face tax
penalties as high as $3,800 a year for not complying,
singles $950. As one resident of Massachusetts where
Mitt Romney imposed an individual mandate in
2006 put it in a Journal story yesterday, this is like
taxing the homeless for not buying a mansion.

"Another Health-Care Invention," *Wall Street Journal*,
October 15, 2009

In the end, the debate over Obamacare—a debate that is still going on—is about the most basic principles of the free market: scarcity
and choice. Scarcity is what gives things value; choosing one option
over another is how we express our own values.* In a free market, the
way we allocate scarce goods (which is pretty much everything) is by
price. When people choose to buy something at one price and not at
another, they are (as we free-market types say) "voting with their
wallets." Any argument over the way we buy health care—pills, doctor visits, surgery, wheelchairs, and those inedible meals they serve in
hospitals—that forgets that all of these things are scarce isn't just
anti–free market; it's antireality.

However, that actually describes not only the Affordable Care Act
but the entire health-care industry. Because most of the prices charged
by doctors, pharmacies, and hospitals is paid by someone other than
the person who actually uses their services, price signals don't really
communicate very much. When you need an appendectomy—as I
did only a few months ago—you don't shop around for the best price,

---

* For more on scarcity, see chapter 2.

partly because, well, you *need* an appendectomy, and partly because you don't pay for it: your insurance does.

What this means is that a whole bunch of very scarce health-care goods are allocated by something other than price, which is by definition inefficient. There are a lot of arguments about how much people should be using price to make health-care decisions, since the alternative to rationing by price is rationing by . . . someone else. You can either recognize this or you can be the *New York Times*:

> Critics have charged that this sensible idea would lead to rationing of care. (That would be true only if you believed that patients should have an unbridled right to treatments proven to be inferior.)
>
> "Reform and Medical Costs," *New York Times*, November 15, 2009

> The battle over women's health care emerged after a federal advisory committee recommended recently that younger women should not routinely have mammograms but should first consult with their doctors. . . . Its judgment was seized upon by Republican scaremongers as an example of the kind of "rationing" that would allow government bureaucrats to deny insurance coverage of important health procedures.
>
> "Senate Health Care Follies," *New York Times*, December 4, 2009

On the other hand (I'm tempted to say the "right" hand), there's the *Wall Street Journal*:

> President Obama objects when people use the word "rationing" in regards to government-run health care. But rationing is inevitable if we simply expand government control without fixing the way health

care is reimbursed so that doctors and patients become sensitive to issues of price and quality.

"Government Health Plans Always Ration Care,"
Wall Street Journal, June 25, 2009

And so it goes. It's hard, if not impossible, to tell whether the positions taken by the *New York Times* are so consistently wrong out of ignorance, denial, or a deliberate attempt to gloss over problems that get in the way of the newspaper's Progressive agenda (this is actually a problem with most Progressives). But whether it's electoral results, climate change, financial regulation, or health-care reform, the last two pages of the paper's first section—where the *Times* makes its editorial positions plain—are one constant in a changing world. If the compass is supposed to point north, you can rely on the *Times* to direct you south.

In testing a statistical hypothesis, scientists—really, everyone—should be on the lookout for two kinds of error: Type I errors, or false positives, are essentially seeing something that isn't there; false nega-tives, or type II errors, happen when you fail to see something that is there.

When both occur at exactly the same time, there's a good chance you're reading an editorial in the *New York Times*.

Epilogue:
The View from 2011

Writing this book (okay, thinking about writing this book) started in early 2009 with the inauguration of President Obama. It ended—sort of—with the midterm elections that "refudiated" (I love that word), more than anything else, his economic philosophy.

This whole thing began with one nervous father: nervous about the widespread acceptance of Progressive ideas and especially the uncritical way they were being presented to my children. If you've gotten this far in the book, you know that I recognize that Progressivism has been around, in the United States anyway, for a century, so it's not that I blame everything about its popularity on the current administration. However, from early 2009 to the middle of 2010, it looked a lot like we had arrived at some sort of Progressive nirvana: a government takeover of health care; management of virtually the entire financial industry; *ownership* of more than half of the domestic automobile business; and, of course, close to a trillion dollars in "stimulus" spending that mostly amounted to a gigantic subsidy of the country's public employee unions while *increasing* the nation's unemployment rate

The second half of 2010, however, was a different story: the rise of the Tea Party movement, huge declines in the president's approval ratings, and, of course, the midterm elections, which turned a seventy-six-vote Democratic advantage in the House of Representatives into a fifty-nine-vote Republican majority . . . the biggest change in more than sixty years.

So I should be less nervous now than when I started, right?

Wrong.

As 2010 turned into 2011, our representatives in Washington were attempting to deal with a couple of, shall we say, urgent bits of business. The first was the expiration, at year's end, of the tax cuts originally passed during the administration of George W. Bush. On December 6, congressional Republicans and the president agreed to extend both the Bush tax cuts and federal unemployment benefits, while reducing the taxes that just about everyone would pay into Social Security and Medicare for 2011. It was an expensive gesture: nearly $900 billion in taxes foregone. Almost all of the money—eight dollars in ten, by some estimates—was aimed at people earning less than $250,000 a year. For Progressives, it was Christmas.

Sure it was.

Calling the Progressive response to the compromise—which it was; no one got exactly what they wanted—hysterical is an understatement. Congressman Jerrold Nadler (D-NY) called the Republicans a "bunch of gangsters." Richard Trumka, president of the AFL-CIO, called it an "unconscionable giveaway." Bernie Sanders, the Senate's only (admitted) socialist, gave an eight-and-a-half-hour speech in which the nicest thing he called the deal was a "moral outrage." Michael Capuano (D-MA) was so peeved that he said that President Obama "may or may not be" the Democrats' best candidate for 2012, a tantrum that was endorsed by such Progressive icons as Keith Olbermann and Ralph Nader.

Why the over-the-top rhetoric? Because in addition to preserving the tax cuts for "ordinary" Americans, the deal did the same for the rich—you know, the people and small businesses that report income in excess of $250,000 a year. The most productive members of society. The ones who do all the hiring and investment. Yup, them.

Or that's how it was reported, anyway, even by reporters who should have known better. The actual compromise didn't tax *people* at different rates; it taxed *income*. Which means that even the richest Americans pay the same tax on their first $250,000 of income that everyone else. But never mind; it's not exactly news that Progressives can't understand tax incentives.

So Progressives, who had been screaming for a second stimulus for months, responded to a deal that would have been—in the words of conservative columnist Charles Krauthammer, the "largest stimulus in galactic history"—by stamping their Progressive feet and threatening to take their Progressive ball home. The reason was that Progressives don't just stand for a reflexive mistrust of the free market; they stand *at attention* when it comes to redistributing income— and that means that anything that didn't punish the wealthy just had to be evil.

Here's how bad it got: I found myself defending the president on *Squawk Box*.

The second, and probably more significant, policy controversy of the end of 2010 was kicked off by the publication of several different plans for reducing the staggering difference between the amount of money that the federal government was obliging itself to spend and the amount of money that the American taxpayer was willing to pay for those obligations. The deficit-reduction plan, first floated by a bipartisan presidential commission, actually showed how it was possible not only to eliminate the ongoing deficit but also to put Social Security back in the black.

The Progressive response? Nancy Pelosi called it "simply unacceptable." It "told working Americans to drop dead," according to Richard Trumka. Paul Krugman said that the commission had been "hijacked."

Yeesh.

Near as I can tell, the reason for such hostility to the Bowles-Simpson plan (named for the commission's chairmen, one a Democrat, the other a Republican) was the way it "gutted" Social Security. It did this—I swear—by increasing the age at which Americans could receive their full retirement benefits from sixty-five to sixty-seven—*seventy-five years from now.*

Progressivism may be hysterical, but it isn't in retreat; it's on the attack. And it retains a powerful set of channels for communicating its philosophy, including television, newspapers, and the Internet.

Oh, and the schools.

Toward the end of the 2010 school year, and therefore the writing of this book, Blake brought home a writing project for her fifth-grade class entitled "Understanding Environmental Concerns." Here's a sample:

> Today you read about the environment and the importance of our country's natural resources. Currently a conflict exists between people who want to reduce the amount of chemicals in the air in order to protect the environment, and those who say it hurts business if we limit the amount of emissions they release.

Now, if you're going to load a question for a bunch of ten-year-olds, you couldn't really do much better than this: The conflict is between people who want to protect the environment and those who want to help (or at least not hurt) business. Environment or business: Pick one.

Here's part of what Blake wrote in response:

> Although I am an environmentalist, in this argument I support the business side. I agree that limit-

ing the amount of emissions a company can release would hurt business. If a company was told to limit its production, it would make less goods, reducing the money it makes. If a company cannot make money, it cannot employ a lot of workers! This would end up hurting the economy, and the unemployed people.

She goes on to propose a compromise involving frequent testing to make sure that soil, plants, and animals are not harmed; and encouraging the company to use its profits to develop greener ways of operating its factories.

It may not be easy to raise a fifth-grade capitalist in twenty-first-century America. But it can be done. Just ask Blake.

Acknowledgments

This book began with a confession: that I haven't really had all that much to complain about during my life. The reason is that I've been extremely lucky. Part of that luck was to be born into the most affluent and freest society in human history—something that every American should probably give thanks for at least once a year.

But most of my luck has appeared in the form of other people, and I'd like to recognize a number of them.

First, Bill Rosen has been an invaluable researcher and collaborator; this book wouldn't have existed without him.

I'm grateful to Mark Hoffman, president of CNBC, for his support and for allowing me the freedom and opportunity to write *Your Teacher Said What?!* Brian Steel and Nik Deogun have blessed the project and offered valuable advice in its creation.

Every day, I'm grateful for the chance to work with a bunch of extraordinary professionals on *Squawk Box*, and I hope this will make up for all the times I forgot to say so to Becky Quick and Carl Quintanilla, my coanchors for most of the last decade; to our executive producer, Matt Quayle, and our vice president of business news, Jeremy Pink. Also, thanks to Todd Bonin, Anne Tironi, Rob Contino,

Matt Greco, Mark Haines, David Faber, Larry Kudlow, Rick Santelli, Ron Insana, Bill Griffeth, and Susan Krakower.

A special thanks to longtime friends Ron Meyer, Peter Foss, Rick Cotton, Jack Schneider, and David Zaslav.

To my mentors, the people who gave me so many opportunities to earn a living in the world of television: Jack Welch (and his wife Suzy); Jeff Immelt; Bob and Suzanne Wright; Jeff Zucker. Thanks also to my former boss at CNBC, Roger Ailes (and his wife Beth); Bill Bolster; Neil Cavuto; and Jonathan Wald.

Blake has a special thank you to offer her friends and—yes—her teachers, for though this project was always intended to remedy some of the gaps in the way she's been taught how the free market works, she's been the lucky beneficiary of a first-rate education in just about everything else, and that matters, too—a lot.

It's likely that readers will notice that this book depends a huge amount on the reporting of others. Much of their work is cited in the endnotes, but a few deserve special notice: my friend and frequent *Squawk Box* guest Steve Forbes, whose magazine and books are practically a road map to free-market philosophy, much of which I've channeled over the last year. The same is true for the editorial pages of the *Wall Street Journal* and the magazine *Reason*, and I'm grateful to their respective editors, Paul Gigot and Nick Gillespie, as well as the dozens of contributors whose thoughts are on display in dozens of places throughout this book. Barry Habib was a huge help in explaining the ways of modern unions. Even more is owed to writers and thinkers whose work has long survived them: Milton Friedman, Friedrich Hayek, Joseph Schumpeter, and—the father of them all—Adam Smith. (And thanks, of course, to Paul Krugman and Frank Rich, both never-ending sources of inspiration.)

The staff at Sentinel has been a joy from start to finish, and I'm grateful beyond words that this book has been in their care: Thank you, Adrian Zackheim, Jillian Gray, Amanda Pritzker, and Will Weisser—and thanks to my representatives at William Morris Endeavor, Eric Simonoff and Ari Emanuel, for brokering this particular match.

Most of all, Blake and I are grateful to the rest of our family: Janie, Chris, Preston, Suzanne, and Margaux Scott; the Kernen dogs, Reagan and Pongo (and Rudolph, the Russian tortoise who will out-live all of us); and most of all to son and brother Scott and wife and mother Penelope. Not only could we not have done it without you; we wouldn't have even wanted to.

Joe Kernen and Blake Kernen

Notes

CHAPTER ONE: JANUARY 2009:
THE PROGRESSIVE SLOT MACHINE

6 "accelerate the desirable process": John B. Parrott, "Obama and Herbert Croly," *American Thinker*, March 27, 2010.

6 "Don't go into corporate America": Byron York, "Michelle Obama: "Don't Go into Corporate America," *National Review*, February 29, 2008.

6 "I, like most of the American": Julianna Goldman and Ian Katz, "Obama Doesn't 'Begrudge' Bonuses for Blankfein, Dimon," *Bloomberg BusinessWeek*, February 10, 2010.

8 A study by the Federal Reserve: Sam Allgood, et al. "Is Economics Coursework, or Majoring in Economics, Associated with Different Civic Behaviors?" *Federal Reserve Bank of New York Staff Reports*, no. 450, May 2010 (available at http://www.newyorkfed.org/research/staff_reports/sr450.pdf).

9 "lower interest rates": Joe McGowan, "Signs of Trouble," *Time for Kids*, January 23, 2008.

13 A professor of psychology and economics: Joseph Henrich, et al. "In Search of Homo Economicus: Behavioral Experiments in Fifteen Small-Scale Societies," *AEA Papers and Proceedings* 91, no. 2 (May 2001): 73–78.

14 "When the greater part": Peter J. Dougherty, *Who's Afraid of Adam Smith?: How the Market Got Its Soul* (New York: John Wiley, 2002).

CHAPTER TWO: FEBRUARY 2009:
THE ABCS OF THE FREE MARKET

16 "way too gullible": Jeffrey Miron, *Libertarianism from A to Z* (New York: Basic Books, 2010).

16 "In 1922, when the U.S. gross": Galbithink, "Annual U.S. Advertising Expenditure Since 1919" (available at http://www.galbithink.org/ad-spending.htm).

25 "perennial gale": Joseph A. Schumpeter, *Capitalism, Socialism, and Democracy* (London, Allen & Unwin, 1976).

25 America had more than 100,000: Michael Cox and Richard Alm, *The Concise Encyclopedia of Economics* (Indianapolis, IN, Library of Economics and Liberty, 2008).

36 None of them is bigger: Daniel Michaels, "As Boeing Hits Turbulence, Uncle Sam Flies to Its Aid," *Wall Street Journal*, December 10, 2009.

41 "What we want is not": Robert Heilbroner, *The Worldly Philosophers: The Lives, Times, and Ideas of the Great Economic Thinkers* (New York: Simon & Schuster, 1992).

46 "lucky fools": John V. C. Nye, "Lucky Fools and Cautious Businessmen: On Entrepreneurship and the Measurement of Entrepreneurial Failure," *Research in Economic History* 6 (supp. 1991).

48 "incroaching on one another's property": Adam Smith, *The Glasgow Edition of the Works and Correspondence of Adam Smith*: *Lectures on Jurisprudence* (London, Clarendon Press, 1976).

CHAPTER THREE: MAY 2009:
THE PROPERTIES OF PROPERTY

60 North America's bison population: Dale F. Lott, *American Bison: A Natural History* (Berkeley: University of California Press, 2002).

CHAPTER FOUR: OCTOBER 2009:
WHO MADE MY SHOELACES?

78 Only at the last stop: This description is taken from a Web site (http://www.enotes.com/how-products-encyclopedia/shoelace) that is a lifesaver for anyone with a curious nature or, more to the point, a curious child. The specifics come mostly from the Artur Mueller Company and the St. Louis Braid Company.

80 "the order brought about": David Boaz, *The Libertarian Reader: Classic and Contemporary Readings from Lao-tzu to Milton Friedman* (New York: Free Press, 1997), citing Hayek, *Law, Legislation, and Liberty*, vol. 2.*The Mirage of Social Justice* (Chicago: University of Chicago Press, 1976).

81 "an invisible hand to promote": Adam Smith, *The Wealth of Nations* (New York: Knopf, 1991).

CHAPTER FIVE: DECEMBER 2009: *WALL-E-CONOMICS*

87 a lot of people had been: Daniel Engber of Slate.com points out quite a few: Daniel Engber, "The Underdog Effect: Why Do We Love a Loser?" Slate.com, April 30, 2010.

87 rooting for the team: Jimmy A. Frazier and Eldon E. Snyder, "The Underdog Concept in Sports," *Sociology of Sport Journal* 8, no. 4 (December 1991).

87 underdogs have a bigger return: Ibid.

88 the same phenomenon caused them: Joseph A. Vandello, Nadav P.

Goldschmied, and David A. R. Richards, "The Appeal of the Underdog," *Personality and Social Psychology Bulletin* 33, no. 12 (December 2007).

93 the dumbing down of American: I'm grateful to Gennady Stolyarov at the Ludwig von Mises Institute for his essay "WALL-E: Economic Ignorance and the War on Modernity," *Mises Daily*, July 4, 2008.

97 *Avatar* is simply the most: James Bowman, "Avatar and the Flight from Reality," *New Atlantis* no. 27 (Spring 2010).

98 the second-most-abundant element: Colby Cosh, "Oil's Not Peaking. It's Jumping the Shark," *Macleans*, April 13, 2010.

99 "for purposes of convenience": Alfred Marshall, *Principles of Economics* (London: Macmillan, 1890).

100 movies and TV shows that depict: For more, see Christina M. Cohn and Lawrence W. Reed, "Free-Market Movie Moments," *Mackinac Center for Public Policy*, June 1, 2007.

CHAPTER SIX: MAY 2010: AMERICA VS. EUROPE

106 the measurable differences between: Denis Boyles, "Vive la Difference: A Review of *The Narcissism of Minor Differences* by Peter Baldwin," *Claremont Review of Books*, Spring 2010.

109 the idea that the United States is less generous: Steven D. Levitt, "Who Spends More on Social Welfare: The United States or Sweden," *New York Times*, May 10, 2010.

109–10 Even after spending fifty years: From the CIA's World Factbook and author calculations; 2009 per capita GDP in terms of purchasing power parity puts France at $33,000, Germany at $34,000, and the United States at $46,000.

112 After a typical immigrant household: Olaf Gersemann, *Cowboy Capitalism: European Myths, American Reality* (Washington, DC: Cato Institute, 2004).

113 In Germany, for example: Ibid.

113 The one time costs of setting: Ibid.

116 German courts even hold: Ibid.

116 In Italy, everyone employed: David Segal, "Is Italy Too Italian?," *New York Times*, August 9, 2010.

116 "workers who can afford": Gersemann, *Cowboy Capitalism*.

117 an article by the libertarian: Lee Harris, "The Spirit of Independence: The Social Psychology of Freedom," *The American: The Journal of the American Enterprise Institute*, July 2, 2010.

117 In 2006, the Pew Research Center Global Attitudes Survey: Gersemann, *Cowboy Capitalism*.

121 "There is no sense": Segal, "Is Italy Too Italian?."

122 "One of the most important features": Schumpeter, *Capitalism, Socialism, and Democracy*.

CHAPTER SEVEN: JUNE 2010: 99.985 PERCENT PURE: THE PRICE OF REGULATION

126 twenty-six states and dozens: Steven K. Happel and Marianne M. Jennings, "The Folly of Anti-Scalping Laws," *Cato Journal* 15, no. 1 (Spring/Summer 1995).

134 As reported by the invaluable: John Stossel, "Good Intentions Gone Bad: The Problem with the Americans with Disabilities Act," *Reason*, September 2, 2010.

134 "The Coast Guard is not": Patrik Jansson, "Top Five Bottlenecks in the Gulf Oil Spill Response," *Christian Science Monitor*, July 1, 2010.

136 In Detroit, however: Louise Radnofsky, "A Stimulus Project Gets All Caulked Up," *Wall Street Journal*, September 21, 2010.

137 designed to get rid of: Harold L. Cole and Lee E. Ohanion, "How Government Prolonged the Depression," *Wall Street Journal*, February 2, 2009.

141 "all of this is about food": William Neuman, "Group Seeks Food Label That Highlights Harmful Ingredients," *New York Times*, October 13, 2010.

142 "to convince consumers to buy": Timothy Gardner, "Cars to Be Graded on Fuel Mileage, Emissions Standards," Reuters, August 31, 2010.

142 "charged with an electric power": Ibid.

142 the cost of federal regulations: Olaf Gersemann, *Cowboy Capitalism: European Myths, American Reality* (Washington, DC: Cato Institute, 2004).

143 President Reagan presided over: Ibid.

CHAPTER EIGHT: AUGUST 2010:
THE $40 OSTRICH EGG

146 the current average U.S. hourly wage: Bureau of Labor Statistics, "Average Hourly Earnings for All Employees and for Production and Nonsupervisory Employees, by Industry, 2009" (available at http://www.bls.gov/opub/ted/2010/ted_20100408_data.htm).

146 the average U.S. family: Actually, 10.6 cents. USDA Economic Research Service, "Food CPI and Expenditures" (available at http://www.ers.usda.gov/briefing/CPIFoodandExpenditures/Data/table7.htm).

146 Today that family spends: Ibid.

147 By 1947, when supermarkets were still a curiosity: Ibid.

149 organic food offers no nutritional: Robert Paarlberg, "Attention Whole Foods Shoppers," *Foreign Policy*, May/June 2010.

149 *E. coli*—whose incidence: Ibid.

149 food-borne illnesses are responsible: Paul S. Mead, et al. "Food-Related Illness and Death in the United States," *Emerging Infectious Diseases* 5, no. 5, September/October 1999, and CDC Morbidity and Mortality Report.

151 If Europe tried to feed: Paarlberg, "Attention Whole Foods Shoppers."

154 every one of the fair-trade licensing organizations: Andrew Chambers, "Not So Fair Trade," *Guardian*, December 12, 2009.

154 not permitted to employ: Ibid.

154 "after paying for the co-operative's": Ibid.

155 Fair trade sets a minimum: Jacob Grier, "Libertarians and Fair Trade Coffee," *Liquidity Preferences*, April 13, 2010 (available at http://www.jacobgrier.com/blog/archives/3773.html).

155 "the parts of the world": David Rieff, "Abused by Hope," *The New Republic*, October 19, 2010.

159 (more than 70 percent of African): Paarlberg, "Attention Whole Foods Shoppers."

CHAPTER NINE: SEPTEMBER 2010: LOOK FOR THE UNION LABEL: YOU'RE PAYING FOR IT

170 so modest that you have: For example, studies have shown small positive effects in the cement industry, negative effects in construction, and negative effects on mining and sawmills. Gerald Mayer, *Union Membership Trends in the United States* (Washington, DC: Congressional Research Service, 2004).

172 the curious fact that thousands: Walt Bogdanovich, et al. "A Disability Epidemic Among a Railroad's Retirees," *New York Times*, September 20, 2008.

172 More than two-thirds of the highest-ranking officials: Steven Greenhut, "Class War: How Public Servants Became Our Masters," *Reason*, February 2010.

173 one FDNY lieutenant retired: Daniel Foster, "Cops and Robbers," *National Review*, August 30, 2010.

CHAPTER TEN: DECEMBER 2010: LIES, D***ED LIES, AND THE OPINION PAGES

190 estimated to cost a bit more: Numbers for the cost of climate change in 2200 are from William D. Nordhaus, *A Question of Balance: Weighing the Options on Global Warming Policies* (New Haven, CT: Yale University Press, 2008). Under Nordhaus's formulas, the cost of capping carbon dioxide at 420 parts per million is between $14 and $20 trillion in current dollars (Jim Manzi, "Conservatives, Climate Change, and the Carbon Tax," *New Atlantis*, summer 2008).

200 Massachusetts congressman Barney Frank "Barney Frank: Fannie and Freddie Must Go," *Investor's Business Daily*, August 19, 2010.

Index

Index